I0461351

UNWILLING OR UNABLE
TO REPORT THE TRUTH

The American News Media
The Assassination of President Kennedy
and How Stories Become History

PENIEL UNLIMITED, LLC

Michael and Kelly Marcades, Publishers
326 Valley Star Drive
Canyon Lake, Texas 78133
Website: http://www.penielunlimited.com
Email: michaelmarcades@gmail.com

PENIEL UNLIMITED, LLC . . . the "author's choice."

The vision of PENIEL UNLIMITED, LLC, as founded by Dr. Michael Glenn Marcades, its President, and Kelly C. Marcades, Technology Director, is to provide superior publishing services for manuscripts worthy of public access. Since its inception, PENIEL UNLIMITED, LLC has taken a particular interest in manuscripts associated with, but not limited to, the assassination of President John F. Kennedy, choral music pedagogy, children's literature, faith-based books, and more.

All rights reserved. No part of this book may be reproduced or transmitted in any form or by any means without written permission from the publisher, except for the inclusion of brief quotations in a review.

Printed in the United States of America

Copyright © 2025, Alex J. Russell

ISBN: 979-8-218-89139-8

This book may be purchased for educational purposes.

All photos are copyrighted and may not be reproduced for any reason without express permission from the owner or copyright holder.

Book Cover Design & Production by Daniel Whisnant (www.suissemade.com)

10 9 8 7 6 5 4 3 2

UNWILLING OR UNABLE
TO REPORT THE TRUTH

The American News Media
The Assassination of President Kennedy
and How Stories Become History

By Alex J. Russell

Published 2025 PENIEL UNLIMITED, LLC

There is no room in America for thought control of any kind, no matter how benevolent the objective.

Jim Garrison
New Orleans District Attorney
1967

TABLE OF CONTENTS

ACKNOWLEDGMENTS

For my family

—

Contemporary writers like myself are forever indebted to all the talented, dogged, and courageous researchers and authors who have come before; who added their effort, insight, and intelligence to what is now a staggering body of work; and who have built a veritable castle of truth and independent thought worthy of that brief period in U.S. history fondly known as "Camelot." That body of work still stands – resolute and permanent – in stark contrast to the Warren Commission and its final Report. It is with immense gratitude and respect for them all, past and present, that this book was conceived.

AJR

OVERVIEW OF KEY NAMES AND TERMS

President John Fitzgerald Kennedy

The 35th President of the United States, John Fitzgerald Kennedy, was famous long before his assassination. His murder was a tragedy that, just as President Kennedy's accomplishments, had contributed to his legacy and lasting cultural impact. A WWII hero, an author, a crusading Senator, and the youngest President in American history – for many people, of different walks of life, this man represented the "New Frontier" – a fabled, future-forward age focused on progress, optimism, peace, and exploration. Since his death, he is often remembered as a proponent of international diplomacy, scientific advancement, and African American Civil Rights.

Like with any man, and especially any President, there were facts and qualities about John Kennedy that were seen as unsavory, unbecoming, and perhaps even criminal: his extramarital affairs; his father's long, checkered history; and, particularly, the 1960 presidential election, which, some contend, was ultimately and illegally stolen from Kennedy's competitor, Richard M. Nixon. To this day, President Kennedy (his name popularly, and affectionately, abbreviated as simply "JFK") remains an icon of a turbulent era in American history and politics, a time in which "the old" clashed with "the new," proponents of violence and bigotry thrashed against those who adopted the ways of nonviolent resistance and civic disobedience, and the world's two superpowers seemed to teeter on the brink of total war.

As a political, social, and cultural symbol, President Kennedy would go on to represent a special kind of American leadership, both at home and abroad – leadership imbued with intelligence, diplomacy, and a regard for all of humanity's endeavors and hardships. The circumstances surrounding his death – as well as those relating to how his assassination had been investigated by the government, and reported on by the press, over time – represent a dark mark on American history and culture. To this day, President Kennedy's assassination – one of the most pivotal events in U.S. history – continues to be grossly, and willingly, mischaracterized and misunderstood.

Lee Harvey Oswald

Despite a mass of counterevidence, reliable testimonies, and thorough, verified research, Lee Harvey Oswald is still *officially* considered to be the sole perpetrator of one of the most infamous murders in American history: the assassination of President Kennedy. He has also been blamed for the mysterious shooting death of Dallas Police Officer J.D. Tippit, who was killed on the same day as the President: November 22, 1963. Oswald – a former Marine; an (apparently) outspoken admirer of Communism; and now, forever cited as the assassin of a U.S. President – had defected to the Union of Soviet Socialist Republics (USSR) in October of 1959, only to return to the country of his birth in June of 1962, bringing with him his Russian wife and small child. After returning to the United States, Oswald would take on a revolving assortment of odd jobs and become acquainted with a variety of suspicious individuals

– chief among them George DeMohrenschildt, an oil geologist living in Texas and whose connections within the spheres of politics, business, and high society have left a sizeable, conspicuous trail. In addition to DeMohrenschildt and the individuals Oswald knew in New Orleans, there are many other confounding and, at times, conflicting aspects to Oswald's short life.

Texas School Book Depository

The sixth floor of this now-famous building was declared to be the site of Oswald's "sniper's lair," from where he allegedly fired three shots at the Presidential motorcade using a traceable, mail-ordered Mannlicher-Carcano rifle (a poorly made Italian weapon known for its inaccuracy). Oswald's alleged crime famously constitutes some of the greatest sharpshooting in history, as none of the expert riflemen subsequently tasked to recreate and test the supposed firing sequence were able to pull it off – even with the added benefit of a stationary target and readjusted scope.[*]

---

[*] Author Craig I. Zirbel thoroughly examines the fallacies baked into the notion that Oswald was responsible for President Kennedy's death in his book, *The Texas Connection*, reviewing the chronology of the tests conducted by the Federal Bureau of Investigation (FBI), as well as the disingenuous approach used by the Warren Commission, in which they attempted to make the facts fit their story, as opposed to having their story fit the facts. While Zirbel's book succeeds in many ways and makes for a helpful introduction to the assassination, there is one aspect in which it fails: it ignores details surrounding Oswald's training at Atsugi Naval Air Facility; the details of his trip to the USSR and

Dealey Plaza

The area in Dallas, Texas, through which the presidential motorcade passed on November 22, 1963. Dealey Plaza is home to the now-fabled "grassy knoll," where many think the fatal headshot that struck the President originated. (Many of the witnesses at the time of the assassination reported hearing shots coming from the direction of the knoll – there are numerous, publicly available, verifiable sources that corroborate this observation.) The abundant and trustworthy witness testimonies regarding gunshots coming from the direction of the grassy knoll – suggesting the presence of a second or even, perhaps, a third shooter – have long been a thorn in the side of the official theory.

The Zapruder Film

Abraham Zapruder, a local businessman, filmed what is perhaps the most famous, if not the most consequential, home movie of all time, catching the moment President Kennedy is slammed back in his seat just after the impact of the fatal headshot. Despite its clear depiction of what had to be a shot from the front of the motorcade – likely coming from behind a fence situated on top of the grassy knoll – the film's veracity has been contested by various researchers and even some Warren Commission critics. However, despite questions surrounding its provenance and authenticity (rumors of tampering have circulated after the fact), the

---

the implications surrounding it; and the potential connections between Oswald and the FBI and CIA.

Zapruder film is generally still considered an important and impactful visual artifact.

Warren Commission Critics

Those who do not trust or believe the findings of the President's Commission on the Assassination of President Kennedy – often referred to as simply "the Warren Commission" – are typically, albeit loosely, grouped together as "Warren Commission critics." The Warren Commission, in its 1964 Report (officially titled *Report of the President's Commission on the Assassination of President John F. Kennedy*), delivered to President Lyndon B. Johnson, among a flurry of journalistic pomp and adoration,[*] declared that Oswald had acted alone and that there was, in the end, no conspiracy. Critics of the Commission's findings have included film directors, celebrated authors, journalists, government investigators, public servants, and ordinary people. Some of these everyday individuals have earned the respect and admiration of fellow critics, having worked hard to support the expanding community of researchers and investigators.

---

[*] In his introduction to Mark Lane's hard-hitting, brilliant book, *Rush to Judgment*, professor and historian Hugh Trevor-Roper characterized this response as "almost universal," adding that, "to dissent was heresy, and journalists – many of whom seem only to have read the convenient 'Summary and Conclusions' which were printed before the text and published separately by the *New York Times* – vied with each other in their praise."

Mary Ferrell was one such person. A key point of contact for countless individuals seeking her resources, help, and insight, she diligently reviewed seemingly endless masses of declassified government documents and helped many to separate reality from obfuscation. A foundation exists in her name, dedicated to the organization and preservation of all the declassified documents pertaining to President Kennedy's assassination. A comprehensive and easy-to-use resource, the Foundation's document database can be accessed online at www.maryferrell.org.

U.S. House of Representatives Select Committee on Assassinations

Established in 1976 to investigate the assassinations of President John F. Kennedy and Martin Luther King, Jr., the House Select Committee on Assassinations (HSCA) began as a serious effort to make up for the egregious shortcomings of the Warren Commission and its Report. The HSCA, in its own final report, ultimately found that President Kennedy "was probably assassinated as a result of a conspiracy." The lifespan of the HSCA is a fascinating story. Many of its members and staff, particularly investigative reporter Gaeton Fonzi, conducted their work in good faith, seeking real answers to serious questions. However, excessive bureaucratic oversight and other recurring obstacles and difficulties curtailed the HSCA's efforts and produced findings that, at best, did not fully support nor confidently dismantle those of the Warren Commission's.[*]

The "Magic Bullet" Theory

Developed by Warren Commission assistant counsel Arlen Specter, the single bullet hypothesis, largely derided for its illogical, improbable conceits and derisively called the "magic bullet" theory, rests on the existence of a nearly pristine bullet found on a stretcher at Parkland Hospital the afternoon of the assassination. This is, and always has been, a contentious piece of evidence, to say the least. Specter, and by extension the Commission, would declare that this particular bullet, supposedly fired from Oswald's Mannlicher-Carcano, had entered President Kennedy's neck, then somehow managed to make its way into the body of Texas Governor John Connally (Connally, along with his wife, was seated in front of the President and his wife, Jacqueline, in the slow-moving limousine). Then, after magically switching direction inside the Governor's body, and exiting out his torso, the bullet then shattered the Governor's right wrist and, finally, ended up lodging itself in his left thigh.

---

[*] Fonzi detailed his time with the HSCA in his excellent book *The Last Investigation*. Widely considered to be one of the best books on the assassination, it is an immensely detailed and eminently readable account of the HSCA's existence, as well as an important recontextualization of the entire subject.

A blatantly improbable trajectory for any bullet to follow – through multiple layers of skin, flesh, and bone – only to come out in near-perfect condition (not to mention the change in direction!), this was, nevertheless, a key component of the Commission's conclusion and a premise that was used to buttress the official verdict. Oswald's guilt was cemented and made official in no small part by Specter's "magic bullet" hypothesis.

A BASIC CHRONOLOGY OF THE ASSASSINATION

Dallas, Texas – November 22, 1963

President Kennedy, his wife Jacqueline, Texas Governor John Connally, and the Governor's wife, Nellie, rode together during the Dallas procession in an open-top limousine, with the Kennedys riding in the back of the vehicle and the Connallys situated in the jump seat directly in front of them. "An estimated 200,000 people lined the roughly 10-mile route" to the motorcade's final stop, the Dallas Trade Mart. "As the motorcade turned southwest on Elm Street and began traveling through Dealey Plaza" – passing the Texas School Book Depository – shots were heard. This occurred at about 12:30 p.m.[*] and was witnessed by scores of bystanders and passersby, many of whom had gathered along the parade route to see the President.

Depending on the source, there were between three and five bullets[†] fired in Dealey Plaza that day. Officially, there were

---

[*] Britannica.com was used to develop this condensed chronology of the assassination. It is interesting to note how Britannica at least characterizes Lee Harvey Oswald as the "accused killer," while Wikipedia, likely the go-to source for many Americans, ignores legal and moral nuance and simply states that President Kennedy "was fatally shot from the nearby Texas School Book Depository by Lee Harvey Oswald." It is fascinating and troubling what a big difference just a few words can make.

[†] Henry Hurt's thoroughly researched and eloquently written book, *Reasonable Doubt*, does a particularly wonderful job of

three bullets, allegedly fired by Oswald from a sixth-floor window of the Texas School Book Depository. According to a broad appraisal of the assassination, however, there is strong reason to believe there were at least five bullets fired that afternoon, from more than one direction. With one bullet bouncing off a nearby curb; objective evidence often conflicting with the Warren Commission's exhaustive but ultimately flawed and misleading report; and scores of witnesses either testifying or commenting that they had heard shots from different directions – notably, from the direction of the fence on the "grassy knoll" – it becomes clear that this amalgamation of facts and first-hand accounts all coalesce into a version of the assassination that is much closer to the actual truth – and yet farther away from what has been, over time, decided to be the truth.

Following the violence and commotion along Elm Street, the Presidential motorcade "rushed to nearby Parkland Memorial Hospital," where the President was declared dead at 1 p.m. Governor Connally had survived his wounds. Shortly after President Kennedy was pronounced dead, and Lyndon Johnson was sworn in (aboard Air Force One, at the time still parked on Love Field, in Dallas), the Presidential party, Johnson's wife and associates, and Jacqueline, her dress streaked with her husband's blood, all flew back east to Washington, D.C.

---

exploring the witness testimonies and physical evidence from Dealey Plaza, from the moment of the assassination to the immediate aftermath. Chapter 4, beginning on page 61, explores ballistic details, as well as the history of the "magic bullet."

President Kennedy's Puzzling Autopsy

The late President had his autopsy performed that night at Bethesda Naval Hospital in Bethesda, Maryland. As with nearly every major aspect of the assassination, the autopsy is infamous for many reasons, including how it was conducted, by whom, and what occurred afterwards. Navy Commanders James Humes and J. Thornton Boswell, assisted by Army Lieutenant Colonel Pierre Finck, were the three men charged with carrying out this most important autopsy. Their processes, results, and testimonies decades after the fact have been consistently challenged by scores of assassination researchers, authors, and medical professionals. To wit, a troubling and unanswered question remains to this day: why did Commander Humes, the leading physician at the President's autopsy, burn his original notes after arriving home from Bethesda? Another kink in the narrative: why was the autopsy not performed by experienced forensic pathologists but was instead conducted by three military doctors who had little experience with gunshot wounds?[*]

---

[*] There are many sources on this, but for those interested in a deep dive into the autopsy, this author recommends either Henry Hurt's *Reasonable Doubt* or Jim Marrs' *Crossfire: The Plot That Killed Kennedy. Trauma Room One: The JFK Medical Coverup Exposed*, by Charles Crenshaw, M.D., with J. Gary Shaw, D. Bradley Kizzia, J.D., Gary Aguilar, M.D., and Cyril Wecht, M.D., J.D., also presents a fascinating look at the autopsy, as well as a fascinating example of unscrupulous infighting among medical professionals. Dr. Crenshaw, one of the doctors at Parkland Hospital who worked to save both President Kennedy and Oswald, published a book in the early 1990s detailing his

experiences. His assertions, contesting the official story, were viciously attacked by some of his colleagues. However, many of the doctors and nurses who worked with him then, as well as other professionals, like Cyril Wecht, had come to his defense by sharing their experiences and corroborating his statements.

INTRODUCTION

This is not a comprehensive account of the assassination or the subsequent investigations. There are countless books, articles, and documentaries that delve into both, some of which are cited throughout. The express purpose of this book is to examine the nature of the American news media – how people consumed it, particularly around the time of President Kennedy's murder; how people interact with it today; how the media has influenced our culture's understanding and perception of the assassination; and what people can do to strengthen their media literacy and become better equipped to identify those instances in which a news story, or even a book review in a news magazine, attempts to propagate blatant falsehoods about the assassination, about Lee Harvey Oswald, and about the significance of this entire story.

This is something that affects most news outlets, regardless of their actual or perceived political affiliations, their stated dedication to the practice of objective journalism, or their professional histories and reputations. (And yes, online publications and blogs, operating outside the processes and norms of the news industry, may make the same errors, consciously or unconsciously.) This book, however, primarily focuses on major U.S. news outlets and publications, including CNN, MSNBC, the Associated Press, and *Time* Magazine.

While the 60-plus years that have since passed do not make for fertile investigative ground, there are always benefits to be found in taking a step back and reexamining something of this scale and magnitude – because, in the end, President Kennedy's assassination *was* a monumental event. It was monumental for America and the world at large, sending shockwaves throughout governments, cultures, and the global news services. As will be discussed in later parts, the assassination and its subsequent investigations constitute not only a dramatic narrative but a grave injustice. There are lingering questions and doubts, even today. They exist not just for Americans, but for the world. For Americans in particular, the assassination represents a kind of cultural wound, a pain point that continues to sting. It is a wound that only the truth can heal.

A sizeable portion of this book focuses on the story of William S. Walter, a man whose experiences before and after the assassination form a concrete and stunning example of how the bureaucratic structures of both the news media and the federal government can, whether actively or otherwise, work against the individual. Walter's story is a lesser-known chronicle, centering around a lost piece of evidence that, in its absence, continues to create meaning for those who do not, cannot, and will not concede that Oswald acted alone – or that he had acted at all. Having explored Walter's story for over a year, this author will continue to dig for any remaining information that may be uncovered. Walter is no longer with us, having passed away in 2021; consequently, reflection and input, direct from the source, are not possible. Having encountered Walter's piece of the larger story in several books, so far, only a handful have treated his experiences with adequate attention; most others are satisfied with providing a few paragraphs.

While it is a portion of the overall assassination narrative that may be considered too limited in scope by some, it nevertheless possesses its own illuminating qualities. In the end, there is always more to learn – even about a topic as specific as this one. Walter's story is a curious set of circumstances, concerning the alleged existence – and subsequent disappearance and cover-up – of a government document warning the FBI of a potential assassination attempt on President Kennedy in Dallas, Texas. In its own way, Walter's story also serves as a quiet warning: be wary of the battles you choose. As the country's relatively short history has shown, a singular person's words and experiences typically matter very little – sometimes not at all – when placed against the towering, oiled, and ready machines of bureaucracy, the federal government, or even the corporate news media.

My own personal interest in the assassination of President Kennedy, my research, and this book represent how new generations, people whose parents were young or not even born at the time of his death, can become invested in the subject. This subject is vastly bigger than us; it is an engrossing, at times daunting, search for truth. It is also its own unique universe of connections, rabbit holes, and unanswered questions. It is perhaps America's most sophisticated mystery, spanning topics as diverse as covert intelligence, the history of the Cold War, the Mafia, the military-industrial complex, forensic pathology, and many others, with all of these areas interlinked in complex, sometimes opaque ways. However, once your interest in the assassination starts to grow, once reading one or two books on the subject is not enough, and once countless hours are spent online, exploring countless documents and message boards, then the weight of President Kennedy's death – its totality – cannot be minimized or ignored. It is this weight that, in part, ultimately motivated the creation of this book.

PART ONE: THE ASSASSINATION AND THE MEDIA ESTABLISHMENT

The Murder and Its Impact

The assassination of President John F. Kennedy on November 22, 1963, is a historical fact. It is also nearly 62 years removed from the present moment. To many, especially those who did not live at the time or who are aware of only the cursory details, President Kennedy's murder is just another historical anecdote, with its own set of facts and personages. It is no more a tragedy to many people today than Pearl Harbor, or the internment of Japanese Americans during World War II. Many such comparisons can be made.

Emotions tied to these and many other events throughout American history – emotions like confusion, fear, and outrage – inevitably become diluted over time. That is only human nature. However, there are always those who, for one reason or another, care deeply about their chosen subject – and there is always a reason why that subject is picked in the first place. Sometimes, however, it seems that it happens in reverse: that the subject chooses the person. This applies to Pearl Harbor, the internment of Japanese Americans, the assassination of President Kennedy, and a plethora of other consequential, complicated, and emotionally loaded events.

President Kennedy's murder is a unique event for many reasons. It is both a contentious topic and a subgenre for various industries, like film and publishing. It can be summarized in a few paragraphs in a history textbook or explored and analyzed in hundreds of books and articles. In this way, the assassination can take on different weights and even different meanings for different people. There are those who attempt to write off the continued doubts and questions surrounding the assassination as basic human curiosity, or perhaps the inability of some people to just accept the unpredictable and random nature of life – that sometimes, bad things happen to people without any real reason; that sometimes, people do bad things just because they can.

This rationale – of letting the past be, of simply accepting events at face value – was, in fact, a major component of the very first official investigation into the assassination. Carried out by the President's Commission on the Assassination of President Kennedy – better known as the Warren Commission, so nicknamed after the Commission's Chairman, Chief Justice Earl Warren[*] – that first investigation was a massive, intensive, popularized, and yet highly secretive process. The Commission held its hearings behind closed doors, employing many staff, interviewing dozens of witnesses, and incorporating a large cross-section of official

---

[*] Earl Warren was "the most respected figure in the American judiciary," wrote Trevor-Roper in his introduction to *Rush to Judgment*. Speaking to the internal workings of the Commission, Trevor-Roper added that: "The Commissioners, being mainly active politicians or administrators, were naturally somewhat irregular in their attendance … No member of the Commission was constant in attendance, although the Chairman scarcely ever failed."

opinions and findings, notably those of the FBI and the agency's director, J. Edgar Hoover.

Created by President Lyndon Baines Johnson, the Warren Commission – which, in addition to Chief Justice Warren, was comprised of Senators Richard Russell, Jr. and John Sherman Cooper; Representatives Hale Boggs and Gerald Ford; the (at the time) former Director of the Central Intelligence Agency (CIA), Allen Dulles; and the (again, at the time) former President of the International Bank for Reconstruction and Development, John J. McCloy – would go on to determine, officially and, they hoped, definitively, that Lee Harvey Oswald* acted alone. It was, in some ways, an attempt to spur the country to move on from what had happened – to move past the enormous shock caused by the President's brutal murder by sniper fire, as well as Oswald's own murder, the latter having been broadcast on live

---

* A lot can and has been said about Lee Harvey Oswald. While this book does not focus on Oswald – many, many narratives have since been written about his life – it is important to state the basic facts: he was a former U.S. Marine who had been stationed at Atsugi Naval Air Base in Japan; he had renounced his American citizenship in 1959 and defected to the Soviet Union; he returned from the Soviet Union to the U.S. in 1962 with his Russian wife, Marina, and their baby daughter; he had been employed at various businesses since his discharge from the Marines; and, finally, he was gunned down by Dallas nightclub owner Jack Ruby in the basement of Dallas Police headquarters, never having received a trial or proper legal representation. In effect, his side of the story died with him.

television. It was also, however, a strong attempt to move past all the lingering questions and doubts.

In a televised response to an NBC report – that was created, in part, to undermine his investigation into the possible New Orleans connections to the assassination – Jim Garrison, District Attorney for New Orleans Parish, explained that one of the Warren Commission's "stated objectives was to calm the fears of the people about a conspiracy." Garrison thoroughly disagreed with this approach, saying that "in our country, the government has no right to calm our fears, any more than it has, for example, the right to excite our fears." In a straightforward presentation highlighting some of the Warren Report's major fallacies, Garrison, with his trademark dry humor and direct manner, emphasized that "there is no room in America for thought control of any kind, no matter how benevolent the objective." (Garrison's 27-minute, taped response to NBC's report is available to be viewed for free on YouTube.)

A Note on Jim Garrison

While he is not the focus of this book, he will reappear throughout. As such, it is important to elaborate briefly on Garrison and his contributions to assassination research. A physically imposing District Attorney known for his sardonic sense of humor, he was the subject of (typically unfavorable) national headlines that sought to cast grave aspersions on his investigation into the assassination.[*] Having found links to the assassination that emanated from New Orleans – links which he and his office could not ignore – Garrison's years-long investigation would eventually lead to an indictment of a prominent New Orleans businessman named Clay Shaw. The trial ultimately ended in Shaw's favor, and Garrison's standing (at least outside New Orleans Parish) would suffer greatly. It was not until Oliver Stone's 1991 film *JFK*, which reintroduced Garrison's work to a new generation, that he was again a part of the national assassination dialogue.

---

[*] Garrison's investigation – as well as some of the major players from New Orleans that were connected to the District Attorney's case, like staunch anti-Communist pilot David Ferrie, Lee Harvey Oswald, and businessman Clay Shaw – was dramatized in *JFK*. Depending on who one speaks to, Oliver Stone's 1991 film is either a historical fiction powerhouse or a misinformed piece of propaganda. In fact, much of the mainstream press attacked the film, attempting to squash its momentum with audiences and critics. The movie nonetheless succeeded, becoming a big hit and influencing the creation of the President John F. Kennedy Assassination Records Collection Act of 1992, which in turn established the Assassination Records Review Board (ARRB).

While there are those who saw the entire trial as a sham, done at the expense of Shaw and his reputation so that Garrison could supposedly achieve some fictional "higher office," Garrison's efforts led to the first public screening of the Zapruder film (which Garrison's office had to subpoena from Time Life). It is also worth noting that the passage of time revealed a great deal about Clay Shaw – information that Garrison and his investigative team had suspected but could not prove at the time. (For those interested in learning more about Garrison, this author strongly recommends Joan Mellen's excellent book, *A Farewell to Justice: Jim Garrison, JFK's Assassination, and the Case That Should Have Changed History*. It is a meticulously researched examination of the District Attorney's entire investigation, as well as an eviscerating reappraisal of Shaw and his connections to the assassination.)

A Note on the Zapruder Film

It is difficult now, as it was when first made publicly available in the late 1960s, to refute the incontrovertible stark power of the home movie filmed by Dallas businessman Abraham Zapruder in Dealey Plaza on November 22, 1963. Available for viewing on YouTube, it clearly shows the killing shot that struck the President in the head, causing him to slam backwards in his seat. However, just like the broader history of the assassination, the history of the Zapruder film is in itself fairly complicated and mired in controversy.

Rumors of tampering and falsification have plagued it for decades[i], as well as the blatantly false and infuriating perspective, propagated by some, that the Zapruder film in fact corroborates Oswald's guilt because, apparently, the President's backward slump in his car seat "could have been a neurological spasm" caused by a headshot from the Texas School Book Depository – the location of Oswald's alleged "sniper's lair" – situated *behind* the President's motorcade.[ii] This, of course, is patently preposterous.

Author Henry Hurt, in his book *Reasonable Doubt: An Investigation into the Assassination of John F. Kennedy*, cites in full what the House Select Committee on Assassinations (HSCA) attempted to sell to the American public: "According to the Select Committee report, the expert [testifying before the HSCA] concluded that 'nerve damage from a bullet entering the President's head could have caused his back muscles to tighten which, in turn, could have caused his head to move toward the rear.'" However, outside of this individual's testimony, the HSCA was not able to provide a full – or convincing – counter-explanation to what is visibly the impact of a bullet fired from *in front* of the motorcade, not from behind.[*]

---

[*] For a more detailed account of the Zapruder film, its history, the controversies that have surrounded it, and what can still be learned from this key piece of evidence, this author recommends the in-depth article "Bedrock Evidence in the Kennedy Assassination" by Josiah Thompson, which can be found online on the Mary Ferrell Foundation website.

Over 60 Years of Journalistic Misrepresentation

Shortly following the assassination, and for years afterward, nationwide polls have reflected how a majority of Americans had continued to suspect that some kind of conspiracy existed which had led to the President's murder – that it was not the sole responsibility of a single, maladjusted loner named Lee Harvey Oswald. While interest still exists in the assassination today – reflected in the various new articles, books, and documentaries being produced, as well as recent discussions in the media about the material declassified by the Trump administration – the passage of time, among other things, has contributed to a marked diffusion in the assassination's resonance and emotional impact.

Despite the 60-plus years of evidence and corroborated testimony, which to this day comfortably and objectively contradict the official story, major news outlets and publications – like CNN, the Associated Press, USA Today, and *Time* Magazine, among many others – continue to propagate and assert the now-debunked allegation that Oswald acted alone. This is, of course, disheartening – even frustrating – but not altogether surprising.

Why This Story?

Why does the news media continue to treat President Kennedy's assassination in this manner? Aside from the fact that different federal agencies and interests have in the past influenced the media and continue to do so (there are documented examples of this[*]), something else should be considered, too. For many people, something like the assassination of a U.S. president is simply too big–too nebulous to handle – especially when compared to their daily demands, concerns, and responsibilities. In a way, this is the perfect story for the news media to undercut, compartmentalize, and, over time, distort.

Even though interest in the truth persists, the media's recurring insistence on Oswald's guilt falls into the same dynamic that Garrison cautioned Americans about in 1967 – that misguided, or even insidious, objective to "to calm the fears of the people about a conspiracy." With this in mind, mixed in with the journalistic mishandling of key ideas, President Kennedy's assassination has also become a sort of national taboo. It was a loaded topic from the start, even before the Warren Commission's Report, and it will likely continue to be a loaded topic for decades to come. The question must be asked, then – why? Why must this topic still be approached from such a distance? Why must there be so many layers of misinformation involved?

---

[*] The assassination story is replete with examples of writers, authors, and reporters with CIA connections injecting themselves into different situations and investigations, often affecting the outcome of said investigations. Gaeton Fonzi, in his brilliant book, *The Last Investigation*, provides a brief overview of this dynamic, highlighting connections between writer Edward Jay Epstein and the CIA. *Family of Secrets: The Bush Dynasty, America's Invisible Government, and the Hidden History of the Last Fifty Years* by Russ Baker is another book that examines this dynamic.

The Information Age

President Kennedy's assassination took place during the early part of the "Information Age." While much of the technology and practices that people relied on in the 1960s may seem antiquated in contrast to what is available today, information nevertheless moved around the country and the world faster and more efficiently than it had before. Since then, the processes through which information is shared have only gotten faster, and the technologies behind those processes have grown sleeker and more sophisticated. Thanks to the then-modern marvels of television, radio, and the teleprint machine, people across the United States, virtually within the hour, knew that their President had been murdered. (Walter Cronkite's historic declaration, during a CBS breaking news bulletin, stating that the President had been shot and killed in Dallas, has since become an iconic moment in the history of broadcast journalism.) Soon, the entire world knew about President Kennedy's fate.

Today, thanks in part to social media, news stories can reach consumers even faster. Everyday people are now able to photograph or record a breaking news story and share it with the world, using nothing more than the ubiquitous, pocket-sized "smartphone." World events can be attested to and talked about in a much more direct way, sometimes before the traditional news media has a chance to prepare its coverage. Notwithstanding technological advancements like these, however, the basic relationship between people as consumers and the mainstream news media (ranging from television to print, as well as online news), and vice versa, has largely remained the same as it was in the 1960s. People generally still expect their news organizations, reporters, and preferred media to deliver reliable, factual information on a variety of topics – from national politics and the economy to entertainment and the arts. And news corporations, in turn, rely on consumers to stay in business.

Like many other aspects of consumerism, people tend to stick to news sources they like or trust or have otherwise used for some time, reflecting a combination of habit and brand loyalty. While not a direct comparison, think of those you know who follow a certain sports team or enjoy a particular film franchise; people, by nature, are tribal, and as such, they typically rely on what they know, trust, and enjoy. The same applies to how people engage with the news and what outlets they will continually turn to. Younger generations, on the other hand, can show a different kind of loyalty, displaying strong affinity for a specific social media application, or app, such as TikTok or Instagram.

The traditional news media still factor into the lives of millions of Americans on a daily basis. As a result, the news industry has to work hard to keep up with new trends and formats, as well as an exponential rise in competition. (This is apparent on virtually any news website, where pop-up advertisements may appear without warning, blocking an article, or a video clip may begin playing on its own. Marketers and advertising teams have to account for different tastes, expectations, and a generally more ephemeral attention span.) In a constant struggle to remain both profitable and relevant, news sites have had to undergo major aesthetic and functional changes – changes that oftentimes make the online experience frustrating for users with a more old-fashioned understanding of the news.

Likewise, TV news also must fight for people's time and attention. Realizing that the online world is perhaps the last media frontier (outside of virtual reality – but that is an entirely separate topic), select clips and episodes from various programs now usually appear on YouTube and other video-sharing sites, as well as on social media. Showcasing the more attention-worthy samples, appeals to emotion are all but ensured – and are typically preferred over straightforward reporting. All of this is not to say that TV news is unnecessary or worthless, but it can be helpful to understand why this medium, and others, function as they do and, at the same time, acknowledge the often-blurred line between journalism and entertainment.

It is a complex sociological matter that, at its core, deals with people's lifestyles and expectations. As in basic economics, with its tenet of supply and demand, so in journalism, we see that as attitudes change, and as the pace of life becomes quicker, and as competition grows, the news industry as a whole has had to not just inform but also divert and entertain. Knowing this, even in broad terms, can help individuals parse through the excess "noise" and get more out of contemporary, mainstream journalism. Because ultimately, for all its faults, there remains a lot to be gleaned from it – if approached correctly and with due care.

Conspiracy Theories and Conspiracy Facts

Those today who do not subscribe to the still-official verdict that Lee Harvey Oswald was the motiveless lone assassin are essentially brushed aside a few feet to the left of what is considered objective reality.[iii] In fact, the theories that spawned in the wake of the assassination represent perhaps the first major instance in which the now (typically) derogatory terms "conspiracy theory" and "conspiracy theorist" were used within the context of American pop culture, soon finding their way into popular entertainment and, expectedly, the news media. Warren Commission skeptics – researchers, writers, respected public servants, and everyday people who do not believe that Oswald acted alone – are not *yet* considered to be equal with those who attest to UFO abductions or Bigfoot sightings. There is, however, a sense that it will not be long until that is so.

The concepts of conspiracy and conspiracy theory have, of course, existed long before mass market paperbacks about crop circles or ghostly encounters. In the most basic sense, a conspiracy is "an unlawful, harmful, or evil plan formulated in secret by two or more persons."[*] Ask someone off the street, and they will likely turn to the cultural understanding of "conspiracy theory," that it is something that has more to do with lonely, paranoid people and less with the real world. However, conspiracy theories are not automatically baseless or irresponsible, contrary to what society has been gradually led to believe. Some conspiracies, it must be remembered,

---

[*] Definition taken from Dictionary.com.

had a lasting impact on civilization and world history – just consider the lasting significance of "the Ides of March."

There is a great amount and variety of theories pertaining to President Kennedy's assassination, involving a diverse array of possible culprits and motives – everything from Attorney General Robert Kennedy's efforts against organized crime inevitably forcing the Mafia's hand to the idea that the assassination had, in fact, been perpetrated by vengeful members of the South Vietnamese government. What most of these theories have in common is that they reject the idea that Oswald was the only shooter – or that he had done any shooting that day at all. Despite the abundance of alternate views, it has to be said that many of these theories are not the products of someone's over-developed imagination; they took shape over time, largely due to the many documented facts that had been gradually made available to the public, contesting the official verdict, as well as the credible, verified testimonies of many witnesses, investigators, officials, and other individuals made available in books, through the press, or in released government depositions. All of this has continued to underscore the many proven shortcomings and fallacies of the government's lone gunman theory.

"Conspiracy theory" or "conspiracy theorists" are not dirty words. It is unfortunate that in this supposedly enlightened age of information and technology, there are those who throw around these terms as disparagements or even insults, further creating a divide between supposedly reasonable people and the "crazy ones" who are not to be trusted or taken seriously. This is a readily apparent dynamic today, seen on message boards, on social media, and in articles and books, dividing the large and complicated story of President Kennedy's assassination into two vague, opposing camps: the "fact" that Oswald had "obviously" carried out the crime on his own and the understanding that there are "conspiracy theorists" who choose to "believe" otherwise. This erroneous, myopic, and needlessly bifurcated rationale ignores the fact that the assassination is – especially by now – well beyond the realm of belief or choice. There are assumptions, there are countless lies, and there are facts, and the facts do not support, have not supported, and will not ever support Oswald's guilt.

The idea that those people who express interest in alternate views of the assassination, or those who put stock in certain theories and explanations of the assassination, are but the misguided few exists in many places. One only has to explore online reviews for different books on the subject to see how some customers go far and beyond simply reviewing a book, defiantly extending their criticism towards people they consider less-than for not abiding by the government's verdict. In general, "conspiracy theorist" is the term of choice, used to delineate those who are supposedly rational from those who are apparently not. At times, it is almost possible to sense the disdain with which those two words are typed.

While not presenting or exploring any one set of answers to the assassination, this author believes beyond a shadow of a doubt that Oswald is innocent. This author also believes that there is no place for pulpits in a free discussion, particularly one as important as this one. Those who view "conspiracy theorists" below them display a kind of misguided apathy that is, at best, very limiting and, at worst, dangerous and antisocial.

A Note on JFK Conspiracies

During the 1950s and 1960s, communism was viewed as a central ideological, political, and even physical threat, particularly within the mainstream news media. The theory that the Soviet Union was in some way behind President Kennedy's assassination, since debunked, flourished for a short while thanks to this political climate, fueled by the "emotions of suspicion, hate, and fear." Even though it indeed was a *conspiracy theory*, the idea that America's communist enemy was behind the killing of a president was "for a long time in the early 1960s, one of the most popular accepted conspiracy theories"[iv].

It was not the official story, but because of the "tenor of the times," it was not outrightly cast aside. As time wore on, however, and as tensions between the United States and the Soviet Union gradually lessened, and as the specter of communism was replaced by other enemies and other threats, this particular theory eventually evaporated. Many others, from the completely credible to the entirely outrageous, have remained.

To this day, the potential involvement of some sections of President Kennedy's own government in his violent death has not been ruled out. It has been the subject of countless books, with many serious researchers delving into the actions and secrets of federal agencies like the CIA and FBI; the U.S. military; President Kennedy's political and ideological rivals; and many other facets of "the powers that be," parsing fact and incontrovertible proof from rumor and innuendo.

"The government did it," as an answer to who really killed President Kennedy, has become a kind of cultural shorthand. It acknowledges that our government – either as a powerful, domineering whole, or as separate but interlinked sections of it – can act, and has acted, in ways both unsavory and criminal. While reflecting a deep-rooted skepticism in our government and institutions, this is not a comprehensive or honest conclusion.

For six decades, the classified documents dealing with the assassination carried with them a particular kind of mystique: the sense that all would finally be revealed and understood, *if only* the government would simply declassify everything. As history has shown, the longer the documents stayed classified, the antsier some got. This is a completely understandable reaction. If the stream of bombshell revelations throughout the 1970s alone taught the public anything, it is that some secrets are not only embarrassing to the status quo, but devastating in their scope and immorality. Such secrets are best kept hidden – forever, if possible.

With time, that general distrust in not just the federal government but in the country's bedrock institutions – from the courts to law enforcement and beyond – would, in some instances, appear to be beyond reconciliation; as elemental and steadfast as any other conviction someone might have. From this broad vantage point, it is easy to see how the contemporary litany of both popular and fringe conspiracies could become an entire industry, even a subculture. It is also easy to see why many, as a result, have chosen to discount almost the entire concept of conspiracy theories, not giving any of them a second glance. At times, it is a dichotomy made up of those who "dive in" too deeply or too haphazardly, and those who stay miles away from the water.

However, if one is to approach the assassination, and the circumstances surrounding it – to include all of the key players, the subsequent investigations, the scandals and intrigues, all of which have been documented and analyzed by scores of capable, diligent authors – the conspiracy theories that have since developed about President Kennedy's murder stem, by and large, not just from, 1) a specific historical, shocking, and public, event, but 2) from suspicious behavior attributed to, as well as the avowed wrongdoings and criminal actions undertaken by, representatives of the U.S. government or its agencies.

"The government did it" is, if nothing else, a gross generalization and oversimplification of the details that have been uncovered and verified over the span of more than 60 years. Just like those who are satisfied with the official verdict, there are those who will only go as far as that, conceding that the federal government may have had something to do with it. As disheartening as history can often be, distrust and suspicion of one's government can only be a starting point, not a state of mind, not something that anyone should resign themselves to. In the context of President Kennedy's assassination, this is a starting point that has borne abundant fruit.

The Soviet Union is no longer a serious suspect. There are still many others – large and powerful ones – who have yet to be cleared beyond any shadow of a doubt.

How We Consume Media Has Changed

Today, people in America and all around the world can stream music, television shows, and movies on their computers or TVs; watch video game playthroughs, Twitch streams, and TikTok videos on their phones; and play video games both online and on a wide variety of consoles, among many other options available. This media explosion is unprecedented in human history, and analyzing this unique phenomenon could fill dozens, if not hundreds, of individual books and research papers.

In the 1960s, some people owned TVs; many still actively listened to the radio; and films, for the most part, could only be seen in movie theaters. In 1963, when President Kennedy was murdered, people got their news via newsprint, over the radio, or on TV. There were only three major networks at the time – ABC, CBS, and NBC – with Americans having to rely on experienced professionals, like Walter Cronkite. Real-time news* and online updates are a given today, but in the 1960s, the news did not happen as quickly. With the advent of the smartphone, major world events can be captured by everyday people and shared instantaneously with a global audience. (It is interesting to imagine President Kennedy's assassination taking place now – the amount of first-person, amateur coverage would likely be overwhelming.)

In his book, *JFK: The CIA, Vietnam, and the Plot to Assassinate John F. Kennedy*, L. Fletcher Prouty writes that "through an intimate new medium known as television, moving pictures on an ongoing war [in Vietnam] were brought into the homes of millions of Americans for the first time. Families also watched while Sen. Joseph McCarthy detailed the internal threat of Communism in government and industry. The public viewed the scenario directly…" It is this direct exposure to the significant events of the 1960s – perhaps the most socially and politically impactful decade of the 20th century, at least for America – that has, over time, evolved into something even more intimate.

Today, it is possible to stay "connected" to the world and what goes on in it virtually 24/7. One does not need to tune

---

* Oswald's murder by gunshot, in this case clearly and undoubtedly perpetrated by Dallas nightclub owner Jack Ruby, was a first of its kind for American news – live murder, televised nationwide. There is no doubt as to Ruby's guilt; however, his motivation for killing Oswald has been the subject of continuous debate. This partly stems from questions surrounding Ruby's presence in the basement of Dallas Police headquarters at precisely the moment of Oswald's transfer from his holding cell at Police headquarters to Dallas County Jail.

in for a special broadcast or sit through commercials. The Internet, smartphones, and other technologies and services have exponentially increased the effects that television – now an almost antiquated piece of technology by comparison – had on American consumers near the middle of the previous century.

But all of this is a general view of the industry and of the technology that has helped shape and transform it. After graduating from college with a degree in visual art and design, this author worked for a little over two years in journalism, holding a combination of freelance, part-time, and full-time roles for a local, independent newspaper. As this was a paper focused on the issues and events of its immediate community, with occasional stories taking on a broader, sometimes national perspective, this was journalism in a unique yet varied microcosm. As such, it was an excellent introduction to the profession and its craft, where newswriting, as well as photography and page layout (now done entirely on computers), were learned and practiced.

Since then, this author has continued to write freelance for newspapers, magazines, and other publications, but there is nothing like being part of a weekly newspaper. Stories would range from breaking news in the community and local politics to spotlights of independent businesses and even regional theater productions. Covering a variety of events and community celebrations, interviewing people from all walks of life and professions, and reporting on issues of interest and importance was both interesting and rewarding – and not without its challenges.

One of those challenges, particular to this author, was the continued encroachment and influence of social media on what should have been a straightforward job: reporting the news. Even in small communities across this country, people communicate to some extent via the Internet, whether it be community message boards, email, or Facebook. Like many newspapers and magazines, the stories that were printed were usually shared on the paper's official website; select stories were also shared on its social media accounts.

This, however, worked both ways – at times, the specific language for the stories we ran and their unique "angles," or points of view, would be devised in such a way as to favor a more social media-literate audience. In this push and pull, it was a question not only of tone, but of how "marketable" stories could be. At times, certain words and passages that were forced upon some of the articles seemed, at least to this author, to talk down to our readers. These were words and phrases that may have been soft and pleasant and catchy, but which at times devalued the inherent seriousness of their subject.

This, of course, is not a new problem for journalism. William Randolph Hearst's infamous message to illustrator Frederic Remington: "You furnish the pictures, I'll furnish the war," is often cited as the prime example of yellow journalism in America. Part of an overarching, sensationalist approach, Hearst sought to do his best to antagonize, blow certain events out of proportion, and ultimately have a violent conflict that would sell papers and increase his fortunes. That conflict was the Spanish-American War.

That is a major historical example, but it paints both an effective and unpleasant picture: money and sensationalism (and entertainment value) have often been uncomfortably, even dangerously, entwined with journalism and the news media, partly because of the nature of business in a capitalist system, but also partly because of the simple fact of human nature. As a species, storytelling is a unique aspect of how we communicate and develop community; it is an old art that permeates our history.

In fact, the approach we use to formulate the history of nations and peoples today is vastly different from classical history, which was more like storytelling than fact-based reporting. As such, looking at journalism broadly, the emphasis on fact and dispassionate reporting is also relatively new. It is a practice that, almost in perpetuity, finds itself at the mercy of passing trends, different cultural expectations, and the almighty dollar.

Front Page News

But for now, let us travel back in time and experience the news as if we were opening our newspapers the Saturday after the assassination…

The New York *Herald Tribune* of Saturday, November 23, 1963, ran an arresting front page story: "Kennedy Assassinated – JOHNSON SWORN AS PRESIDENT." Beneath the large headline, there are two photos: one of President Kennedy and his wife, Jaqueline, subtitled "A FINAL WAVE from the President to his fellow citizens," and one of Lyndon Johnson, again with Jacqueline, aboard Air Force One during Johnson's swearing-in ceremony. (As will be discussed later, this second image became a somber, iconic photograph of the end of an era, but as with almost every aspect of the assassination, this singular photo has its own dark caveats.)

This same front page portends to have "THE FULL STORY," starting with "The Assassination" and going all the way to "The Future." Douglas Kiker, of the *Hearld Tribune* staff, wrote that President Kennedy was "shot through the brain by an assassin just as he was completing a triumphant eight-mile motorcade through the streets of Dallas yesterday." Kiker continues, writing that the President was "hit by two rifle shots in the neck and in the right temple." The official count would increase to three shots, according to the Warren Commission. The unofficial, more plausible count typically stops around five.

A seemingly inconspicuous sentence in the early portion of the story, but it already, inadvertently or not, works to plant a dangerous, misleading seed in the readers' minds. Before speeding past the object of violence – the fatal headshot – the story briefly imparts that the President was murdered by "*an* assassin" (emphasis added).

The benefit of the doubt cannot alleviate 60-plus years of similar journalistic misinterpretation, particularly as so many journalists who have since stuck to the theory of Oswald's guilt should know better by now. It may seem like an inconsequential point to linger on, but by this simple arrangement of words – "an assassin" – <u>there now begins a narrative</u>, where there should instead have been the reporting of facts, as well as the open and honest admission of facts that are not yet known – such as who really fired the gun, how many shooters there actually were, where the shots had come from, and in what exact sequence the bullets hit the President. Recall the "magic bullet" theory, which, by its very existence in the official Report of the Warren Commission, put up a smokescreen between the evidentiary truth and the people's right to know this truth. The Warren Commission's fallacies and distortions did not exist in a vacuum.

Kiker's extensive coverage of the assassination includes an interview with eyewitness Mary Norman, "who was aiming her Polaroid camera at the President at the exact moment [he] slumped forward in his seat and then slid down." *Forward*, not backward, the way that the Zapruder film shows; the way numerous eyewitnesses had described that moment.

Kiker also quotes Dr. Kemp Clark, Parkland Hospital's chief neurosurgeon, as saying "'it was apparent that the President had sustained a lethal wound.' He said that 'a missile had gone <u>in and out the back of his head</u>, causing extensive lacerations and loss of brain tissue.'" The direction of the fatal headshot, the number of possible shooters, and several other key considerations are significantly altered depending on how one reads the underlined portion of Dr. Clark's quote.

Again, in the *Herald Tribune*, as in many newspapers across the country, only a few days later, the story of the assassination and its aftermath remained *the big story*. The Monday, November 25, issue of the *Tribune* ran the following front-page headline: "A Nation Appalled." The central photo? The gruesome, since-televised shot of Lee Harvey Oswald at the moment of his own shooting, at the hands of local Dallas night club owner Jack Ruby.

Ruby's back is to the camera as he stands mere feet away from Oswald, whose face is contorted in a gruesome expression of pain and shock. Several law enforcement officers surround the scene, but are pictured almost frozen in their tracks, immobile and useless.

The photo of Ruby shooting Oswald is subtitled with the following: "BULLET STRIKES VITALS of accused assassin Lee Oswald as night club owner Jack Ruby pulls the trigger." The story right beneath this picture, by *Herald Tribune* staff writer Maurice C. Carroll, begins with these grotesque words: "Lee Harvey Oswald met an assassin's death yesterday, just 48 hours and seven minutes after the bullets he was accused of firing killed the President of the United States." An "assassin's death" for someone who never stood trial.

Following the assassination of President Kennedy, Oswald's death, Ruby's criminal, premeditated act, and the funeral procession in the nation's capital, along with other, connected stories, all appeared in quick succession in newspapers across the country, on television screens, and over the radio in countless homes. Words and images have impact; the larger story of the assassination of the President was quickly becoming a new American saga, one full of powerful images, shattered lives, and high drama.

It was an emotionally loaded, charged period. Perhaps this, in part, explains the form and flow of the news coverage at the time, but facts are no less important at a time when fear and passions flare. However, as shown in these examples and throughout this book, the supposedly sacred institution of journalism not only reported but also saw fit to narrate, weaving a story for the American public before the dust had a chance to settle. In short, a wholly irresponsible way in which to treat the lives and deaths of real people.

In a section to the left of the front page story about Oswald's murder, titled "In the News This Morning – From the *Herald Tribune*'s World-Wide Sources," a small segment called "In the Nation" remarks that "The single shot that cracked in the basement of the Dallas City Hall yesterday closed forever the story of the man who the police believe committed one of the century's most incredible crimes." An "incredible" crime? Yes. But "closed forever"? That is an interesting and borderline unscrupulous position for any journalist, living and operating in a free, democratic society, to take – particularly about a story and an event as important and impactful as the assassination of a President and the subsequent murder of the alleged assassin.

In all fairness, on page 4 of the same issue, a story by Martin G. Berck, of the *Herald Tribune* staff, posits that "Oswald

Guilt May Forever Be Questioned." This article considers the fact that, in our society, the accused must stand trial and, in theory and according to our moral norms, is to be presumed innocent *until proven* guilty. But Berck's article, while acknowledging the inherently broken nature of the case against Oswald, also proceeds to ask rhetorical questions that in effect buttress the prevailing suspicions surrounding Oswald's guilt.

One example: "Did the social climate of the United States or of Texas contribute in some sense to the murder of President Kennedy? However demented Oswald may have been, did he need a special atmosphere to propel him?" What kind of question is this to ask, particularly only three days after the murder of the President, never mind the death of the alleged assassin? Keep in mind, a Dallas police officer had also been murdered. His story, however, was in short order overshadowed by items focusing on Oswald and the President.

The *Danville Register*, serving the city of Danville, Virginia, ran a morning issue that following Saturday, November 23, that featured several Associated Press (AP) items – not least a story that proclaimed, "Man Formally Charged With Slaying Kennedy." The first line of this article reads as follows: "Police Chief Jesse Curry said Friday night charges of murdering President Kennedy have been filed against Lee Harvey Oswald." The Dallas District Attorney at the time, Henry Wade, was reported to have said that "the case will probably be brought to the grand jury by the middle of next week." As expected, in a case of this magnitude, things were moving fast. "When asked if there were fingerprints on the gun he [Wade] said he did not care to go into that at the present time."

Another story, also on the front page, also by the AP, reported that "A gunman assassinated President Kennedy from ambush Friday with a high-powered rifle." Whether it was the fast-moving, ever-evolving nature of the facts or the apparently desirable thrust to weave together some kind of narrative that could quickly explain away this compounding tragedy, it is evident that the early news stories did not concern themselves, by and large, with the *unanswered* questions.

In serious journalism, one must always admit to that which is not yet known; to that which the author cannot claim is true or cannot be backed up to be true. But potential holes and open questions were jumped over, avoided, and discarded in the early news coverage of the assassination. This, tragically, became an overwhelming pattern in our fourth estate – something that is still followed today. How was it already certain that there was just *one* gunman? How was it already known for sure how many shots were fired that day? How did the authorities already *know* from what direction the shots had come?

The *Danville Register*'s front page also includes an article by Jack Bell, an "Associated Press White House correspondent, [who] was in the fourth car behind President Kennedy's on Friday when an assassin killed the President from ambush." As anyone can plainly see, it was "*an* assassin" (emphasis added). This was seemingly being drilled into each reader, prior to the conclusion of any official investigation (and remember, this is just the morning after the assassination).

Bell's article, titled "Three Loud Reports – A President Is Shot," clearly did not benefit from the myriad eyewitness accounts that described a higher shot count. In his article, he writes about the warm welcome that the denizens of Dallas bestowed upon the visiting President: "Ironically, if their [the President and his team] reception in Texas had not been so warm, precautions might have been taken to raise the shatter-proof side glass even though the top of the convertible was down. Such protection might have saved the President."

Bell continues: "But Dallas, where the President's policies had raised a storm of conservative protests, had been warm in its welcome to the handsome, bronzed President and his pretty, chic wife." A warm reception? That much was true, but Bell underplays the sense of threat and danger that members of the President's team had cited – both at the time the discussions about a trip to Dallas were first initiated, and later, as preparations were talked over and carried out. This is a well-known fact: the President's trip to Texas was potentially up against far more than just a vague "storm of conservative protests."[*]

---

[*] For those interested in learning more about the details surrounding the President's trip to Texas, this author suggests reading *Reasonable Doubt*, *Crossfire*, and *The Texas Connection*. These books paint a detailed picture of the political and social

50

Among the many examples of this was a leaflet printed by the area's ultra-right-wing conservatives that branded the President a traitor. Titled, in large print, "WANTED FOR TREASON," this handbill accused President Kennedy of such "treasonous activities against the United States" as being "lax in enforcing Communist Registration laws" and appointing "Anti-Christians to Federal office." Ridiculous on its face, but dangerous, nonetheless.

Bell's story continues: "The presidential party appeared to be chatting gaily among themselves after they had left the crowds of downtown Dallas behind, and their caravan had swung into a quiet area where admirers had not chosen to gather. But there the assassin took his stand. His three well-aimed shots plunged America and the world into grief." Well-written and evocative, but again, on what kind of authority does a journalist have the right to weave what can now most assuredly be called a "narrative," and not a news story?

Examining these contemporaneous artifacts, it is both interesting and important to understand the mismatched confluence of information. There are some points of information that have persisted to this day, such as the notion that there was just one shooter, while others were introduced in the early news reports and quickly dropped.

---

atmosphere in Texas – particularly Dallas – as it related to President Kennedy and his perceived policies. They also take the reader "behind the scenes" into the formative stages of the President's fatal trip.

In the previously cited article, "Man Formally Charged With Slaying Kennedy," the AP reported that Dallas police found "the rifle, partly hidden behind some books [allegedly inside the Texas School Book Depository building]. It was a bolt-action model, believed to be of Japanese make, with telescopic sights." Roughly two days later, as evident in the November 25, 1963, edition of the *Herald Tribune*, the alleged rifle of Japanese make had magically transformed into the "6.5 Italian Carbine." A reproduction of the mail-order ad from Chicago's Klein's sporting goods shows the rifle that "Oswald bought." (Even to the uninitiated, there is a difference between weapons made in Italy and those made in Japan; experienced law enforcement officers would be able to identify the basic type of weapon found at the scene.)

In the official narrative, the Mannlicher-Carcano was promptly connected to Oswald as the rifle that he, for some reason, had purchased by mail, something that – long before the age of "CSI" and other shows of that variety, which popularized police procedurals focusing heavily on the science of forensic detection – was easy to trace.

In "Man Formally Charged With Slaying Kennedy," the AP also reported the following: "Police said Oswald worked at the book depository building; had lived in the Soviet Union and married a Russian woman. On Nov. 1, 1959, he had said he was applying for Soviet citizenship. Someone telephoned police just before 2 p.m. that a suspicious character had been seen entering the theater [where Oswald was ultimately picked up, by scores of police], a short distance from where

Patrolman J.D. Tippett had been slain." (The article misspells Tippit's name.)

However, "what caused the slaying of Tippett was not immediately clear. Police said the slaying didn't make sense at first look. By the time police had brought Oswald from the theater, a large crowd had gathered. It was in an ugly mood and had to be held back. Police were *tight-lipped if they had any other evidence* to connect Oswald to the shots that felled the President." (Emphasis added.) Later in the same article, a lot is made of Oswald's "unusual" background. Granted, at the time, his background – his journey to the Soviet Union, his attempt to denounce his U.S. citizenship, his marriage to a Russian woman – *was* unusual. However, the story forgoes further probing into the criminal aspects of the case, opting instead to focus on the "unusual" Oswald.

All of this is not to say that individual journalists – on the national scale, from the AP, and those working for local newspapers, operating in New York City or in Danville, Virginia – had all consciously decided to partake in any kind of purposeful obfuscation. A part of the problem at the time was that whatever the "authorities" decreed or shared was usually taken at face value and accepted as fact. Why would the Dallas police lie to the journalists present? Why would the government purposefully lie to its people about the assassination?

In this way, President Kennedy's death can be seen as a major fulcrum in our history, set between a past in which both the authorities and the news media took part in maintaining the status quo, and a subsequent future in which it became common, even expected, to be suspicious and critical of the government and other powerful institutions (often, it must be said, for good reason). It was nothing short of a seismic shift, affecting the entire country.

While journalism's past may seem, from a modern point of view, suffused with a somewhat gullible mindset, it is important to remain mindful of each unique time period, to examine an era's particular context, general norms, and cultural zeniths. In this way, by objectively and fairly reassessing the nation's social, cultural, and political history, taking care to appreciate a nuanced and well-rounded picture, a greater, more accurate truth can develop. While, in a larger sense, the 1960s were not that long ago, that decade – or any decade – cannot be approached from a purely contemporary perspective. This foregoes study and analysis and instead emphasizes interpretation.

Time Capsule

Part of the reason that these stories were selected and analyzed is that the news reports of that time are an eye-opening, fascinating time capsule. The articles published on the days and weeks immediately following the assassination should not be taken at face value, however – not because the authors had deliberately lied, but because, as showcased above, the objective was not always to report what was and was not known about the assassination of the President, or the murders of Oswald and Tippit, but to tell a story – to reflect the shock and horror that people felt, and, in their own way, provide an epitaph for the Kennedy Presidency.

Various publications made sure to cover the late President's wife, his children, and the extended Kennedy family who were all photographed and written about throughout the mourning period and the funeral proceedings in Washington, D.C. The new President of the United States, Lyndon B. Johnson, was also a key subject, including his dramatic swearing-in ceremony aboard Air Force One, the rumors of his heart attack in Dallas, and the various issues of the day that he was now responsible for. Other famous names made their way into the post-assassination coverage, known around Washington, D.C., the country, and the world, by way of condolences and emotional remarks in light of the tragedy in Dallas. Looking at all of this today, the purpose of many of these articles and stories has more to do with expressing grief, sorrow, and outrage – rather than the adequate analysis of known facts.

In the early days of assassination coverage, there began a fast and hard conflict between the volleys of facts that had been adjusted for mass consumption and those that were closer to the actual truth. At the outset, bits and pieces of accurate information had made their way into the news cycle; even in the pre-digital era, developments about something as massive as the assassination of a president were coming in fast, with some reports overlapping or contradicting each other. The rate at which this happened eventually slowed, and the narrative soon ironed out into a cohesive, but altogether flawed and inaccurate conclusion. The push and pull between fact and narrative, however, continues.

In those early days, even before the Warren Commission had been organized, the (apparently) straightforward answer – one killer, no conspiracy – was being pushed fervently upon the grieving public. "The press," Lane writes in *Rush to Judgment*, "largely endorsed and publicized the Government's position, so that the distinction between wild conjecture and responsible dissent was obscured."[v] However, facts contradicting "the Government's position" did, essentially, slip out in the initial stages. For example, Mary Woodward, "an employee of *The Dallas Morning News*, who witnessed" the assassination "from a location in front of and just to the left of the wooden fence [on the grassy knoll], wrote that 'suddenly there was a horrible, ear-shattering noise coming from behind us and a little to the right.'"[vi] Interestingly enough, not the official source of the shots – the Texas School Book Depository.

The following few pages include photos of pages from the referenced publications; as the central focus is on a visual understanding of page layout and presentation, whole articles are not included. As such, some of the texts may be cut off in places. Bear in mind, these newspapers are very old and worn, purchased by the author for research purposes and in order to include visual examples of what newspapers of the time were like.

This eye-grabbing pairing of history-making images are featured on the front page of the *New York Herald Tribune* (Saturday, November 23, 1963).

A quote from Johnson starts "The Full Story." As this edition was released only a day after, it is rather confounding to find the "full story" in the Saturday edition, and on the front page no less.

The Monday, November 25, 1963, edition of the *New York Herald Tribune* features Lee Harvey Oswald's public execution on page one. Jack Ruby is pictured on the right, his back to the cameraman, gun in hand.

As Oswald's death plays out for the world to see, the news cycle pauses to highlight both the slain President's mourning family and the funeral proceedings in the nation's capital.

A dangerous confluence of hard reporting and commemorative writing, plus speculation, abounds shortly after November 22.

Also in the Monday edition of the Herald Tribune, Ruby gets top billing as the "brooder with crazy bravado," while Oswald's murder is relegated to the bottom half of the page. It is hard to

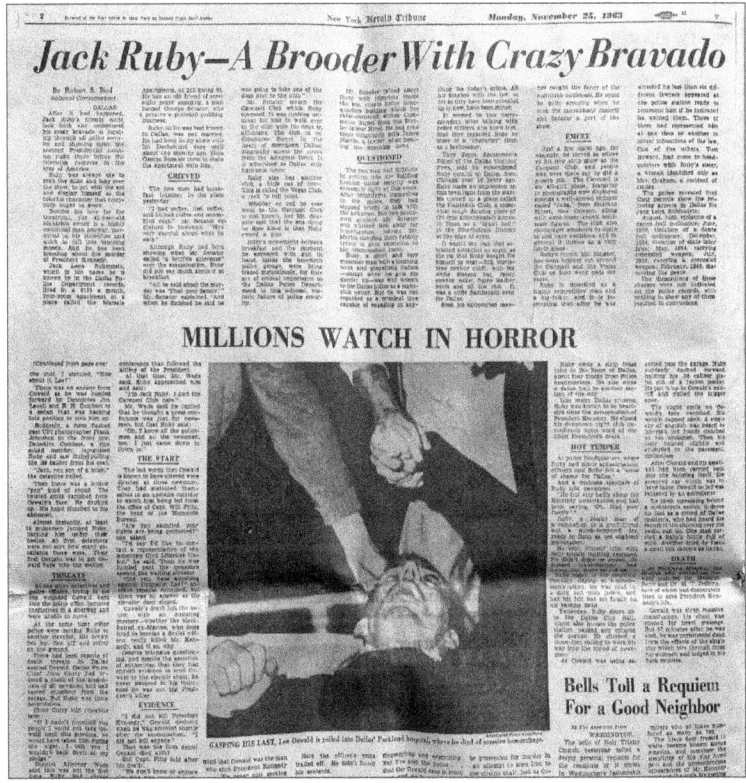

unilaterally blame all reporters and all newspapers of the time, many of whom were undoubtedly caught up in a major, fast-moving story. But with the benefit of hindsight, it is clear how an *emotional* narrative could have blossomed, spurred on by the fourth estate.

In a story as complex and upsetting as this, with developing, compounding horrors – from the President's death, to Oswald's, to this report about Dallas Police Officer J.D. Tippit, a storm of facts, feelings, and interpretations ruled the news cycle. In view of this, it is perhaps understandable – though not forgivable – how quickly much of the mainstream news media celebrated the Warren Commission's final report, claiming an end to the confusion and unresolved questions. (Monday edition of the *Herald Tribune*.)

Kennedy Assassinated

(Continued from page one)

Main and Commerce, out of the main business section, where the crowds were thinning out.

The President's limousine was just turning right and was about to enter Stemmons Freeway for the last lap of his ride to the Trade Mart.

It was here that the shooting occurred. Some witnesses say two shots were fired, others one. The doctors who attended the President at the time of his death say it was impossible to tell.

Mrs. Connaly, who was not injured, described the experience to Julian Read, an aid to the Governor, who then informed the press.

Mrs. Connally remembered that she had just remarked to the President: "You sure can't say Dallas wasn't friendly to you today." She related that the four of them were "all very pleased" about the size of the crowd and the reception.

The first shot, she said, hit the President. When he was hit, she said, Gov. Connally immediately turned to look and was struck in the chest himself.

According to Mrs. Mary Norman of Dallas, who was aiming her Polaroid camera at the President at the exact moment, he slumped forward in his seat and then slid down. She said she screamed, "My God, he's shot."

Mrs. Connally related that Mrs. Kennedy immediately "grabbed the President." She—Mrs. Connally—did the same with her husband, and both women ducked down in the car, shielding the men from further assault.

She said she does not remember the President saying anything on the five-minute, high-speed ride down the freeway to the hospital.

Another eyewitness was a Dallas television news photographer, Mal Couch, who said he saw the rifle being pulled back inside the window of the Texas Book Depository Building. He said that he estimated the shooting was done on the fifth or sixth floors. Other windows in the building were filled with other employees at the time.

Sen. Yarborough, riding behind with Mr. Johnson said, "This is too horrible to describe. This is a deed that is indescribable."

Sen. Yarborough, in a state of shock, described the scene as he saw it. As soon as the shooting happened, he said, Secret Service men "immediately surrounnded the Vice-President's car and sped him away."

On the trip to the hospital, he said, "I saw another Secret Service man in the President's car beating his hand

AT WHITE HOUSE, flag flew at half staff.

Of course, while smaller items focused on the aftermath and various related aspects, top of mind was the national – and global – response to the assassination. Somber images, like the one used here, were circulated to cement the emotional tenor of the time. (Saturday edition of the *Herald Tribune*.)

The Monday edition of the *Herald Tribune*.

A fascinating tidbit, featured in the Saturday edition of the *Herald Tribune*: a historical overview of other infamous Presidential assassinations that had occurred in the U.S. up to that time. A day after John Kennedy is no more, newspapers like this take the opportunity to remind readers that this kind of violent crime has, in fact, happened before. An attempt would be made, decades later, on President Ronald Reagan. John Kennedy's brother, running for President, would also die by gunfire.

These two items, while small, are telling of a sense of unease that would follow many Americans long after the release of the Warren Report. As the graphic in the top center of the page suggests, why would a Presidential assassin order a traceable weapon through the mail? One could have easily been purchased in Dallas, or a nearby city, over the counter – anonymously.

The government of the Soviet Union, perhaps quizzically to some at the time, was in fact deeply concerned about President Kennedy's assassination. Premier Nikita Khrushchev and the President had been steadily developing a rapport unique for that period of the Cold War (it was not a linear sort of progress, but it was important nonetheless). As some researchers have stated, and others postulated, the Soviet Union, for a short time, had been a prime suspect in the President's murder. Cold War animosity and conflict notwithstanding, assassinating the President was the last thing that Moscow wanted.

Lastly, it is important to note that based on 60-plus years of investigative efforts by scores of dedicated men and women, it has become abundantly clear that Oswald's guilt is no longer in question. That is to say, the responsibility for the President's death lies elsewhere.

A Note on the JFK Assassination in Popular Media

It is interesting to note how *The X Files* and *Twin Peaks* – television shows that both began in the early 1990s – had reflected the pervasive cultural shock of the assassination. While vastly different in plot and themes, both shows briefly touched on the subject in their own ways, winking at the audience about the unfinished nature of the case.

In *The X Files*, the theory that Oswald was the only shooter is ridiculed by a trio of computer hackers and conspiracy theorists who publish an underground news journal called "The Lone Gunman." In an early episode, one of the trio (aptly called the Lone Gunmen) reflects on a conversation he had with a shooter who had been positioned on the Grassy Knoll, disguised as a Dallas police officer. Although essentially a throw-away piece of dialogue, this reflects an established theory that has found its way into many interpretations of the assassination, from Oliver Stone's *JFK* to the recently published book *Admitted Assassin* by Ricky White, J. Gary Shaw, and Brian K. Edwards.

In *Twin Peaks*, one of the show's protagonists, FBI agent Dale Cooper, muses into his tape recorder about who really pulled the trigger on President Kennedy. A small moment that is nevertheless unique due to its inclusion in a series that largely has little to do with real-world events and is instead more concerned about dreams, magic, and the concept of good versus evil. (Considering the years of speculation about the FBI's potential involvement in either the murder itself or the resulting cover-up, having an FBI agent ponder what the true answer behind the assassination may be gives the scene an added dimension.)

In the 1997 film *Conspiracy Theory*, starring Mel Gibson and Julia Roberts – in which Gibson plays a New York City cab driver who sees vast conspiracies everywhere – President Kennedy's *alleged* killer, Lee Harvey Oswald, is mentioned several times. Gibson's performance finds humor, tension, and sympathy in his character's story; for Jerry Fletcher (Gibson), the fact that Oswald was not responsible for the President's death is a given. *Conspiracy Theory* also showcases how common it was (and still is) to find that the accepted, mainstream version of the assassination puts all the guilt on Oswald. As opposed to being given the benefit of the doubt and seen as a human being, Oswald is often depicted as some larger-than-life villain, a notorious killer, one of American history's several infamous "lone assassins."[*]

Incidentally, when Gibson's character is on the run from goons dispatched by the film's villain (played by Patrick Stewart), he decides to hide inside a movie theater to avoid

---

[*] While, by now, Oswald's guilt has been sufficiently disproven, it is unfortunate that the lies which continue to sustain his notoriety remain commonplace in the mainstream media.

capture. This must have been a conscious reference to Oswald's real-world movements on the screenwriter's part. In Dallas, shortly after the tragedy in Dealey Plaza, the police, in great numbers, would soon descend upon Oak Cliff (a Dallas neighborhood) and find Oswald inside the Texas Theatre.[*]

Stepping outside of television and cinema, and into the world of ghost hunting literature, one should not be totally surprised to find that even Ed and Lorraine Warren – who had earned a lasting reputation as real-life ghost hunters, demonologists, and paranormal investigators – included a short but emotional reflection on the late President in their 1989 book, co-written by Robert David Chase, titled *Ghost Hunters*. The passage dealing with the memory and legacy of President Kennedy is very brief, but it is nevertheless fascinating that even in a book that focuses on hauntings and the afterlife, one can recognize the lasting imprint that President Kennedy and his assassination had on the American psyche all those years later.

Media Literacy and the JFK Assassination

Media literacy has always been important – for as long as there has been "media" for people to create and consume. But now, in 2025, media literacy is perhaps more important than ever. As opposed to 1963, when people relied on

---

[*] Researchers have spent a long time trying to piece together the truth behind Oswald's decisions on November 22, highlighting specifically the nature and timing of Oswald's identification and arrest.

newspapers, the radio, and their televisions, Americans today must sift through virtually endless sources and perspectives. To someone unaccustomed to today's media culture, it can be a dizzying combination of formats, topics, and ideologies. It is ultimately impossible to remove all bias from journalism and the news media because, after all, human beings are responsible for reporting the news. No individual is free of prejudice or bias of some kind. However, this does not mean that attempts to reduce the effects of this bias – either from "inside" the industry, from the point of view of those who report the news, or from the "outside," meaning the consumer – should be discarded altogether.

Media literacy, as a practice and a skill that can be internalized, rests on the ability to synthesize as much objective truth as possible through a variety of voices and points of view. It can never be satisfactory or beneficial to rely on just one perspective or source – this can be comforting in a basic sense, but is altogether limiting, more akin to tunnel vision than awareness. The world is vast, as are many of its topics and issues, necessitating an approach that fits and responds to the various intricacies of a subject, as well as to the inherent bias in almost every major news organization – however obvious that bias may or may not be. Being able to remain agnostic regarding which sources one uses to stay informed, utilizing multiple perspectives or sources to understand the details of a story, and recognizing the telltale signs of propaganda all play essential roles in improving and strengthening one's media literacy.

Identifying Bias in the Media

The news media do not have to try very hard to muddle simple truths about President Kennedy's assassination. Articles released during anniversaries of the assassination can appear very benign, tame, and simple, existing for seemingly no other reason than to commemorate one of the country's most famous Presidents and one of its most infamous events. However, all it takes is one line of text – referring to Oswald as the culprit[*], for example, or noting that his "assassin's perch" was located on the sixth floor of the Texas School Book Depository – to reveal the inherent shortcomings of such reporting[vii].

The official theory has proven its longevity and prevalence. However, it exists through the precarious circumnavigation of our country's basic legal, journalistic, and moral tenets – that the alleged perpetrator of any crime is innocent until proven guilty, and that facts should decide the outcome of a case, not feelings, impressions, or official statements. A quick check of Oswald's Wikipedia page reveals that this key concept has either been forgotten or that, for some reason, it simply does not apply. While it is true that the deceased cannot be libeled, there is an implicit responsibility to posterity and history that has essentially been cast aside in

---

[*] While this may seem like "splitting hairs," reporting that someone is an *alleged* perpetrator, as opposed to simply saying someone *is* the culprit, is a very important legal, journalistic, and ethical distinction. According to the law, people in America are innocent until proven guilty. Oswald was never proven to be guilty, least of all in a court of law.

this particular – and essential – case, failing Oswald and his family but also, by extension, all Americans.

It is true that justice is never guaranteed. However, individuals have a *chance* at justice under the laws, expectations, and implications of the American judicial system. Oswald's murder by Jack Ruby in the crowded basement of Dallas Police headquarters ensured that justice would forever be denied to the *alleged* murderer of President Kennedy and Officer Tippit. This story, replete with loose ends and unsettled questions, is nevertheless often portrayed to the American people as a case that has been fully investigated and closed. Imagine a wall in your home, full of termite holes – but covered up with wallpaper. The holes are no longer visible, but they are there – and the wallpaper itself is much too thin to stay there indefinitely.

The Way It Was, The Way It Continues To Be

When a book or documentary is released that presents views and facts contradicting Oswald's guilt, and when this new product is covered by the mainstream media – typically through a review or an interview with its creator – this new book or documentary is, at best, presented in the context of entertainment. It is often approached as something that is not entirely fiction, but which falls short of reality. Facts contradicting the official theory are very rarely given the opportunity to form into serious conversations or counternarratives.

The news media comprises "the fourth estate." Beyond reporting the news, honest journalism plays a vital role as a cornerstone of a free and democratic society. Responsible journalism is a fulcrum of our political structure and society, resting on the fundamental premise that informed individuals are better equipped to make their own decisions and form their own views. A democracy cannot function without objective journalism. This is something that has been proven time and again, both domestically and internationally. In a healthy democracy, questions can be asked and pursued honestly and publicly. Why, then, has the assassination of President Kennedy – and, by extension, Oswald – been so terribly misrepresented?

Where in the American press can one find the unfettered flow of ideas and perspectives concerning President Kennedy's assassination? Over the past six decades, credible, responsible people, if not having theorized and investigated the assassination, have at least publicly and lucidly sought to ask incisive, worthwhile questions; these individuals could scarcely be called "crackpots" or brushed off as mere "conspiracy theorists," and yet they have often faced an uphill battle in getting their voices heard.

(There are too many to list here, but some notable critics of the Warren Commission's findings and of the official theory in general include the likes of Cyril Wecht[*], a nationally-

---

[*] Wecht is featured in Oliver Stone's four-part documentary mini-series, *JFK: Destiny Betrayed*, released in 2021. Informative and well-made, it takes time to explore the physical evidence,

known forensic pathologist; Charles Crenshaw[*], one of the several doctors at Parkland Hospital who worked to keep both President Kennedy and Oswald alive; and Pennsylvania Senator Richard Schweiker, a respected Congressman and member of the "Church Committee" who had called for an official reinvestigation into the death of President Kennedy.)

The news industry could provide the public with a great service and make up for what has constituted a decades-long insult[†] to the common sense and intelligence of millions of Americans. If the public forum could finally widen in some meaningful way, if words like "alleged" and "suspected" could finally and permanently enter the lexicon surrounding Oswald and his overt, as well as supposed, connections to the assassination, and if the assassination were no longer

---

particularly in relation to Parkland Hospital, the doctors who had operated on both Kennedy and Oswald, and the "magic" bullet.

[*] Dr. Crenshaw's book, *JFK: Conspiracy of Silence*, co-written by Jens Hansen and J. Gary Shaw is a straightforward account of a doctor who witnessed aspects of the assassination that were not publicly discussed until 1991's *JFK*. Dr. Crenshaw's book was reprinted twice – as *Trauma Room One: The JFK Medical Coverup Exposed* and as *JFK Has Been Shot*. There were those who came out in support of his story, such as forensic pathologist Cyril Wecht, while others in the medical profession attacked Dr. Crenshaw in the news media and in the *Journal of the American Medical Association* (*JAMA*).

[†] Despite the analysis presented here, this author does not encourage or condone a blanket avoidance of the mainstream news media or think that people should mistrust it as a whole. To the contrary, this author recommends a more proactive, responsive, and responsible approach to consuming the news.

treated as something totally and completely solved, there would then be more space for others – journalists, authors, researchers, anyone – to explore this matter with the attention and respect it deserves. The case is not closed, despite appearances to the contrary.

A Note to the Reader

If you are genuinely interested in the history and minutiae of the assassination, do not feel discouraged by some who falsely insist that it is time for the topic to be put to rest. Yes, there are many unfounded theories and opinions on the subject, but there are also numerous rational and well-researched ones. The fact that the assassination of President Kennedy still interests and intrigues people from all walks of life is, of itself, an important fact.

The individual person has a natural nose for lies and truth, and time has shown that many such people were compelled enough to learn more, to discover, and to connect with others who, for one reason or another, sensed or understood that there was more to the story than what had been offered: the legend of a lone, motiveless assassin. In fact, the history of this loose coalition of writers, researchers, professors, film directors, journalists, and many others could fill several books. Undoubtedly, many Warren Commission critics have provided for each other a unique sense of community and camaraderie over the 60-plus years of investigative work.

Americans have lived through various crises and conflicts unique to their time. But those nagging, unresolved feelings that many still have concerning the assassination have persisted through decades of other major events and tragedies. Those feelings, almost certainly, will continue to persist. President Kennedy's murder is packed with emotional and psychological density: the violent death of a popular President; the tumultuous era in which it occurred;

the lack of answers; the palpable reluctance on the part of many in the mainstream news to treat this story with the accuracy and dignity it requires; and a conspicuous, damaging rift between the people and those they elect into power.

As a moment of historical and cultural significance, it has been more or less sequestered along with the rest of our country's history; an event that is no more, and no less, than the sum of America's story – just another chapter in the history books. If not this, then at best President Kennedy's murder is used, along with many other examples, to underscore the social context of the 1960s – a very singular time often reflected on as a period of stark uncertainty, violence, and palpable distrust in the nation's institutions. But a nation's history, or even a portion of that history, is constantly in flux. It is a story with many writers, and it is always being written. Historians are not the only ones who contribute; journalists, elected officials, and even artists all have a say, at one point or another, in how our history is to be told, retold, and perceived. Regular citizens, too, rightly have the same say. It can be easy for many to forget this.

A Note on Dr. Charles Crenshaw

Dr. Crenshaw, in his book *JFK: Conspiracy of Silence*, reflected in 1992 how the Warren Commission – which asserted that Lee Harvey Oswald was the lone gunman, shooting from behind President Kennedy – had seemed "mysterious" to him.[viii] In 1992, almost 30 years had passed since the death of President Kennedy; scores of books had been published on the subject, some gaining national attention and helping to educate the public on the dangerous shortcomings of the Warren Commission. Even so, after Dr. Crenshaw published his book, he was attacked in the media and by colleagues in the medical field.

The notion that there was more than one gunman was still too crazy, too outlandish to stand behind. To many who regurgitated or otherwise stood by the official theory, people like Crenshaw – no matter how respected they may be in their field, how many other likewise respected and trusted individuals back up their story, or how measured and credible their account – represented anything from a frustrating annoyance to a valid threat to the established narrative. In fact, the official theory has been consistently under threat from not just the scores of researchers, investigators, and writers, but by the unadorned, self-evident facts themselves, collected, organized, analyzed, and reanalyzed over a period of 60-odd years.

Even now, many will echo that same flawed sentiment – that there's nothing suspicious or even untoward about the assassination. This passage from Crenshaw's book, however, summarizes something incredibly important: "As I watched the President's loosening grip on life, I had absolutely no doubt that I was viewing two frontal-entry bullet wounds. Had we turned him over, we would have discovered a third entry wound in his back, between the shoulder blades."[ix] Authors J. Gary Shaw and Jim Marrs are among those researchers who, based on interviews and an exhaustive review of the evidence, believe that the actual scenario in which President Kennedy was shot and killed was predicated on having the President finding himself in a crossfire, explaining the wounds that Dr. Crenshaw and the other doctors witnessed – with several of these doctors speaking to, or writing about, their observations after the fact.

Dr. Crenshaw also rips into the Warren Commission's "magic bullet theory," which postulated that "a missile traveled through President Kennedy's neck, then traversed Governor Connally's torso, whereupon it shattered his wrist, and finally lodged deeply within his thigh." Dr. Crenshaw called this scenario out for what it has always been: something "beyond absurdity."[x] In addition to being a first-person account of one of this country's most shocking events – giving readers an insider's perspective of the critical period that soon followed after shots were fired in Dealey Plaza – Dr. Crenshaw's book also explores and dissects that eponymous phenomenon, the "conspiracy of silence." A dynamic built around implicit complicity, with various people, for reasons of their own, choosing to withhold speaking publicly about their experiences, Dr. Crenshaw himself was a part of this conspiracy of silence for many years.

While Oliver Stone's *JFK* may be just a movie – a work of historical fiction, a product of Hollywood, complete with a roster of famous actors and a musical score by none other than an industry giant, John Williams – it nevertheless broke an immense barrier in late 20th century America, influencing Congress to establish the Assassination Records Review

Board (ARRB), and pushing others to tell their stories – just like Dr. Crenshaw did with his book.

A Note on the Support Dr. Crenshaw's Story Received

Mark Lane, in *Rush to Judgment*, wrote: "The doctors who examined the President in Dallas on November 22 observed two wounds: a small wound in his throat and a massive wound in the rear portion of his skull."[xi] (Speaking to the nature of entrance versus exit wounds, Lane explains that "an entrance wound usually has no ragged edges and is small and round and neat. An exit wound usually has ragged edges and is large and elongated."[xii]) The nature of President Kennedy's rear head wound, as recalled by many of the operating staff at Parkland Hospital, fits the description of an exit wound. The other wound that was readily apparent to Parkland staff was a small entry wound in the President's neck (these being the "two frontal-entry bullet wounds" that Dr. Crenshaw referred to in his book).

"The doctor who had conducted the autopsy at the military hospital in Bethesda, Maryland (Commander James Humes), was ordered not to discuss the matter."[xiii] (Humes had gone on record as having destroyed his original autopsy notes.) It was not until the 1990s that another detail emerged. In "The Medical Case for Conspiracy," a segment that was added to the 2001 edition of Dr. Crenshaw's book (retitled *Trauma Room One: The JFK Medical Coverup Exposed*), authors Gary L. Aguilar and Cyril Wecht write: "On August 2, 1998, the *Associated Press* reported an important ARRB (Assassination Records Review Board) finding: 'Under oath [before the ARRB], Dr. Humes finally acknowledged under persistent questioning – in testimony that differs from what he told the Warren Commission – that he had destroyed both his notes taken at the autopsy and the first draft of the autopsy report.'"[xiv]

Speaking further to the destruction and disappearance of critical evidence, the authors note: "All three of JFK's pathologists, both autopsy photographers, a White House photographer, and a National Photographic Center employee have testified that photographs taken at JFK's autopsy are missing."[xv] Drs. Aguilar and Wecht continue: "Witnesses overwhelmingly described a gaping wound in the right rear of JFK's scalp and skull, an area that appears entirely undamaged in the autopsy photographs."[xvi] (In fact, the veracity of the published autopsy photos has long been in question.) In any case, that "gaping wound in the right rear" of the president's head is the same wound that Dr. Crenshaw attested to in his book.

"The Medical Case for Conspiracy" is a fascinating addition to the original text. In addition to providing more context to the medical aspects of the assassination, outlining a more accurate chronology of events, and helping to set the story straight, this chapter also includes a list of medical professionals who corroborated Dr. Crenshaw's account. The list, including doctors and nurses from Parkland, reads as follows: Kemp Clark, MD; Robert Grossman, MD; Ronald Coy Jones, MD; Gene Aiken, MD; Paul Peters, MD; and Pat Hutton, RN.[xvii] Drs. Aguilar and Wecht remind us that, in the end, "the theory of Oswald as the sole shooter requires that myriad witnesses were wrong about the gaping wound in the backside of JFK's skull, including nurses and neurosurgeons in Dallas, and the FBI agents and autopsy surgeons in the morgue."[xviii]

Lane, quoting from a *New York Times* article, explains that "'Dr. Malcolm Perry, an attending surgeon, and Dr. Kemp Clark, chief of neurosurgery at Parkland Hospital, gave more details. Mr. Kennedy was hit by a bullet in the throat, just below the Adam's apple, they said. This wound had the appearance of a bullet's entry.' Four days after the assassination, a doctor who had examined the President at Parkland Hospital again was quoted as stating that the bullet which struck the President in the throat entered from the front: 'Three shots are known to have been fired. Two hit the President. One did not emerge. Dr. Kemp Clark, who pronounced Mr. Kennedy dead, said one struck him at about the necktie not.'"[xix]

In Lane's analysis of the Warren Commission's proceedings, he underscored that when the Parkland doctors "appeared before the Commission or Commission counsel, they were presented with a hypothetical question containing almost the entire case against Lee Harvey Oswald and were asked if it were possible that the wound in the President's throat could have been an exit wound. Several of the doctors indicated that it was rather unlikely." Dr. Ronald Coy Jones, who had made a "handwritten report … on November 23 had noted a 'a small hole in the anterior [frontward] midline of neck thought to be a bullet entrance wound.'"[xx]

Examples like these, ranging from decades ago, nearer the date of the assassination, to the more recent past, such as the 1990s – a decade that brought about a resurging interest in the assassination – encompass a collection of testimonies that readily dispel the Warren Report's core tenet, still adhered to by many in the news media to this day: that Oswald, firing from above and behind the motorcade, was the sole perpetrator. It is especially significant to trace the remarks of Parkland Hospital staff over time, as this lends their perspectives greater credibility and, in light of the other evidence that has been made available, deconstructs the shameful contentions of the Warren Report.

Dr. Crenshaw wrote, "At Parkland Hospital the wound to the right side of the President's head is a large, gaping hole extending from the temple area all the way around to the back of the head [indicating frontal impact]. At Bethesda Naval Hospital [where the President's autopsy that was used by the Commission to buttress its conclusions took place], the back of the President's head is intact, with only a small puncture just to the right of midline near the base of the skull. The large gaping hole is *only* on the upper right side, with no damage to the rear of the head."[xxi]

Taking into account just a small selection of literature focusing on the medical evidence – Dr. Crenshaw's book, the piece titled "The Medical Case for Conspiracy," passages from *Rush to Judgment*, and the Warren Report itself – it becomes clear that following the assassination, there had almost always been at least two opposing sides at play. Before contemplating the possible motives of all the "tainted evidence, manipulated [bullet] trajectories, and a false autopsy,"[xxii] it is vital to acknowledge the recurring, very much conspicuous push and pull between the Commission's narrative and the nonconforming medical facts.

VISUAL GALLERY

Like inside many of the books on the assassination of President Kennedy, on the following pages you will find a collection of photographs dealing with the subject matter at hand. Unlike many of the usual photos, however, these images provide a broad overview of the assassination and the context in which it occurred, serving as a way for those new to the topic to get a feel for the time and place that President Kennedy inhabited – as a living, breathing man before his death, and as a symbol shortly after.

These images are in the public domain, and as such are readily available online and are easy to find. Yet they are often sidelined within the bounds of this particular narrative. There are dozens upon dozens of books that feature images of the President's wounds, to include autopsy photos (their authenticity often the subject of debate among professionals and eyewitnesses), as well as sketches and diagrams. Images of the rifle that the federal government proclaimed was Lee Harvey Oswald's weapon of choice, as well as close-ups of the infamous "magic bullet" are all well-known to virtually millions of readers.

This particular gallery, a "visual interlude" of sorts, offers something different. Many of these photos are included in order to underscore the inherent humanity of the subject matter. Gaeton Fonzi, in his marvelous book *The Last Investigation*, expressed this sentiment best when he wrote that the core of this story dealt with the unjust taking of a man's life. Beyond the fact of this man's role and stature in life, his time on this planet was cut short in the most cowardly, despicable manner possible.

As such, the photos included in this book, snapshots from the President's short tenure in office, as well as photos of the assassination's aftermath and the funeral procession in the nation's capital, serve as a reminder that, next to the mystery and intrigue, next to the decades of leftover confusion and muddled facts, the central issue is this: a man's life was unjustifiably and violently ended. The fact that this man was President of the United States did not, however, guarantee any kind of meaningful action on the part of those who, in positions of equal or even higher power, were left to continue in his stead.

86

Taken by President Kennedy's official photographer, Cecil Stoughton, this is a view of the motorcade as it proceeds down Main Street, approaching Dealey Plaza. The President's limousine, which also included Governor Connally (and the Governor's wife), can be seen in the distance, with Dallas motorcycle policemen riding alongside it. In the subsequent decades, questions would persist about the level of protection the President received that day in Dallas, with several Warren Commission critics pointing out how lax the security presence was.

(Cecil Stoughton, Public Domain.)

DEALEY PLAZA -- DALLAS, TEXAS

1. TEXAS SCHOOL BOOK DEPOSITORY
2. DAL-TEX BUILDING
3. DALLAS COUNTY RECORDS BUILDING
4. DALLAS COUNTY CRIMINAL COURTS BUILDING
5. OLD COURT HOUSE
6. NEELEY BRYAN HOUSE
7. DALLAS COUNTY GOVERNMENT CENTER (UNDER CONSTRUCTION)
8. UNITED STATES POST OFFICE BUILDING
9. PERGOLAS
10. PERISTYLES AND REFLECTING POOLS
11. RAILROAD OVERPASS (TRIPLE UNDERPASS)

An aerial view of Dealey Plaza, as it appears in the Warren Commission Report. After a slow turn off Houston Street, left onto Elm Street, President Kennedy was fatally shot between the Texas School Book Depository building (number "1" on the map) and the railroad overpass, also called the triple underpass (number "11" on the map). Eyewitnesses, many of them having gathered in Dealey Plaza to catch a glimpse of the President, as well as casual onlookers, had gathered along Elm and Main streets, near the grassy knoll, and even on the overpass, overlooking the plaza. The recollections of many witnesses contradict the official story, particularly regarding the number and direction of shots.

(Warren Commission Hearings, Vol. 17, Public Domain.)

In addition to the harrowing sequence recorded by Abraham Zapruder, which can be viewed for free on YouTube, there were many other visual records of the assassination in Dealey Plaza, such as this Polaroid photo taken by bystander Mary Ann Moorman, taken right after a bullet struck President Kennedy in the head. Past the presidential limousine, a section of the famed "grassy knoll" is visible. Although it is a very grainy image, the President's body language here corresponds with his movement in the final frames of the Zapruder film, his body slumping backward against the seat.

(Mary Ann Moorman, Public Domain.)

One of the many photos taken by Stoughton on the day of the assassination, this photo depicts the presidential limousine, parked outside Parkland Hospital, shortly after the events in Dealey Plaza. The limousine remained in the parking lot after the President and Governor Connally were taken inside. Based on first-hand accounts, there was an overpowering atmosphere of chaos.

This can account for *some* of the disorderly handling of crucial evidence, like the limousine itself, which, logically, should have been removed from the scene and inspected for clues. And yet, serious questions remain about how much of the evidence was handled – often in a puzzling or downright improper fashion by both federal authorities and local police. One thing is for sure: the "chain of evidence" procedure was not followed.

(Stoughton, Public Domain.)

A Note on the Chain of Evidence Process

In a typical murder investigation, evidence and key areas must be isolated from any potential tampering. When a piece of evidence is collected, a meticulous record is kept of who interacted with it and when, thereby maintaining the "chain of evidence." Without this process, whatever evidence is collected becomes inadmissible in court. Keeping a clear and detailed record of the chain of evidence involves collecting, transferring, and storing the evidence for practical and legal reasons.

Since, in 1963, the murder of President Kennedy was, legally, the responsibility of Texas police, and not federal law enforcement, the presidential limousine should have been impounded and searched for clues by the Dallas officers. This was not done. The limousine, under typical circumstances, would have been prized as a potentially abundant source of clues and other indispensable information. (For example, studying the bullet marks and holes on the outside and inside of the vehicle could have led to a more accurate and complete understanding of the bullet trajectories.) Instead, the Warren Commission was tasked with recreating the shot trajectory, eventually developing the "single bullet" theory as part of its final answer.

This photograph was taken by Stoughton during President Kennedy's motorcade through the City of Tampa, Florida, on November 18, 1963. (Notice the President, in the back seat, on the right-hand side, in an open-top limousine, just as he would be days later in Dallas. See also the local police presence; there are as many as six officers in this photo, positioned in front of and to the sides of the limousine. Compare this scene to the first photo in this section, which shows, albeit from a greater distance, a markedly reduced police presence.)

Stoughton's proximity here should also be noted, with the photographer evidently following the presidential limousine directly behind – whereas, in the Dallas photo, he is situated roughly four cars away. These are small but telling differences in both the general level of security in both cities and in the vantage point that Stoughton, the President's White House photographer, was afforded during each trip.

(Stoughton, Public Domain.)

Stoughton took many photos of this one event: Lyndon B. Johnson's unusual swearing-in ceremony aboard Air Force One. This is not the more popular shot, which has since become an iconic image of the 1960s, but it characterizes the exact moment with perhaps more nuance and depth – capturing the marked informality of those gathered in the frame.

(Stoughton, Public Domain.)

This is the well-known photograph of Johnson's swearing-in ceremony, included here for comparison's sake. Johnson, with his right hand raised, and Jacqueline, the late President's wife, are framed as the image's central subjects, with several of the other individuals, visible in the preceding photo, blocked from view by Johnson. For better or for worse, this is one of the many images that have gone on to define the decade in which they were produced.

(Stoughton, Public Domain.)

Johnson's arrival at Andrews Air Force Base on the day of the assassination.

(Stoughton, Public Domain.)

Panic, Urgency, Chaos

Cecil Stoughton's photos of Air Force One's arrival at Andrews Air Force Base are not the world-famous frames from the Zapruder film, or even the now-historic image of Jacqueline Kennedy standing by Johnson as he is sworn in as the next President of the United States. Nevertheless, they offer us a unique point of entry into the past, and a palpable sense of what it must have been like to be there. The feelings of panic, urgency, and chaos that were felt in Dallas followed Air Force One east. Johnson quickly assumed his new role as President Kennedy's corpse was transported to Bethesda Naval Hospital for a late-night autopsy.

Note the microphones prepared for Johnson's arrival in the second photo (on the preceding page). President Kennedy's assassination and death would not only make startling headlines around the world, but his lying in state, within the U.S. Capitol Building's Rotunda, and his funeral procession through Washington, D.C., created a dense pall over the national consciousness. In print and on television, the news showcased the solemn grandeur of his funeral, shining a spotlight on the Kennedy family and, in both subtle and obvious ways, positioning them as a kind of American royalty – royalty that had just lost a beloved, influential member of their clan. There were undoubtedly plenty of Americans who disliked both Kennedy the man and Kennedy the President, particularly for his liberal policies regarding social justice, race relations, and the Soviet Union – but in broad terms, his death was a somber episode for many Americans.

With the benefit of hindsight, and years of research into his assassination, there came the chilling realization that – for all the gravitas, the ceremonial weight, and profound sadness that comes with the death of a man and the murder of a popular President – justice would perpetually evade President Kennedy. Long after the contemplative spectacle of his funeral, a time in which leaders from around the world expressed their sorrow and condolences, and long after the seeds of John Kennedy's legacy took root, his assassination remains an unresolved, violent, contemptuous blot on the country, its history, and its future.

The President's caisson leaves the White House among throngs of mourners and onlookers. November 25, 1963.

(Abbie Rowe, Public Domain.)

The evening of the funeral. November 25, 1963.

(Rowe, Public Domain.)

Robert F. Kennedy and his brother, John, at the White House.
October 1962.

There are many key similarities between the assassinations of John Fitzgerald Kennedy and his brother, Robert Francis Kennedy. Both were murdered in public, in front of numerous witnesses. Both murders, naturally, made for big news stories and, historically, represented symbolic turning points for American society. President Kennedy's "lone gunman" was Lee Harvey Oswald, whereas Robert Kennedy's alleged killer was Sirhan Bishara Sirhan. There is a world of questions surrounding President Kennedy's assassination; the same applies for his brother.

President Kennedy was the most powerful and influential man in the world the day he was murdered in Dallas. Robert Kennedy, much like his brother, had also become a public beacon of leadership, symbolizing positive change, unity, and prosperity for all Americans, regardless of race, creed, or stature. Well on his way to winning the 1968 Democratic Primary, Robert's murder occurred on June 5 of that year in Los Angeles, California, at the Ambassador Hotel. It, too, remains a dark mark on American history, politics, and culture.

(Stoughton, Public Domain).

President Kennedy's September 30, 1962, address to the nation regarding the rioting at the University of Mississippi and the deployment of National Guard troops in support of integration in the South.

(Rowe, Public Domain.)

A Note on John F. Kennedy's Involvement in African American Civil Rights

On September 30, 1962, President Kennedy addressed the nation, via television and radio, on a subject that, at the time, was openly and often violently contested in many parts of the country, particularly the Deep South: desegregation. Speaking about the violent rioting at the University of Mississippi, the President explained to the country that the United States was "founded on the principle that observance of the law is the eternal safeguard of liberty – and defiance of the law is the surest path to tyranny...Americans are free, in short, to disagree with the law – but not to disobey it."

While the larger theme of the broadcast was desegregation and African American civil rights, the specific matter was this: segregationists in Oxford, Mississippi, wanted to maintain the long-held, racist practices of keeping white and black Americans separate in virtually every aspect of life, including education. As such, protesters gathered at the University of Mississippi sought to prevent James Meredith, an African American student, from attending school there.

Meredith's enrollment would contribute to integration, something many southerners absolutely did not want or believe in. President Kennedy's bold move to deploy 30,000 National Guard troops to Oxford and put an end to the riots created a path toward widespread integration, and as a result, James Meredith became the first African American student to attend the University of Mississippi. The riots, federal intervention, and the resulting push toward integration coalesced into a historic turning point for the national Civil Rights movement and helped cement President Kennedy's legacy of supporting and defending equal rights in the United States.

27.

U.S. Secret Service
Protective Research Section

CO-2-33,998

SAN ANTONIO OFFICE

DATE OF ORIGIN: November 15, 1963

ORIGIN: Information received telephonically from FBI Headquarters
Washington, D.C.

DETAILS: Subject interviewed by FBI on November 14, 1963, and
stated that he is a member of the Ku Klux Klan; that
during his travels throughout the country, his sources
have told him that a militant group of the National
States Rights Party plans to assassinate the President
and other high-level officials. He stated that he does
not believe this is planned for the near future, but he
does believe the attempt will be made.

BACKGROUND OF
SUBJECT: Subject was arrested on September 30, 1963, in Piedras
Negras, Mexico, with two other men for stealing three
automobiles. Information developed by the FBI indicates
that the subject was attempting to make some sort of
deal with them for his benefit in the criminal case
now pending against him. There was no information
developed that would indicate any danger to the President
in the near future or during his trip to Texas. As of
January 27, 1964, subject was still incarcerated pending
Federal court action.

EVALUATION OF
DEGREE OF
DANGER: In view of subject's incarceration, he was considered
to be of no danger at this time.

ACTION: No further action taken.

SUBSEQUENT
ACTIVITY: None. An FBI report received January 31, 1964, relative
their interview in jail.

STATUS ON
11/22/63: Subject incarcerated.

COMMISSION EXHIBIT 762—Continued

Warren Commission Exhibit 762, found on page 566 in Volume
17 of the Commission's Report, outlines the U.S. Secret
Service memorandum that, in an indirect way, serves to
substantiate – or at the very least, support – William S. Walter's
story. This memo has been featured in the book *Survivor's
Guilt: The Secret Service and the Failure to Protect President*

Kennedy by Vincent Michael Palamara, as well as in an article by the late Professor Donald E. Wilkes.

(Public Domain.)

> Memorandum to Mr. W. C. Sullivan
> RE: ASSASSINATION OF PRESIDENT JOHN FITZGERALD KENNEDY
> 62-109060
>
> 2. Walter would be contacted by United States Attorney's Office in New Orleans and be instructed to utilize the executive privilege in refusing to discuss any matters dealing with his former employment with the FBI. This would be the normal course of action that would be followed in dealing with a subpoena issued to an ex-FBI employee. However, the Department recognizes Walter is a liar who cannot be trusted and that even though he was instructed to use the executive privilege he very well, when questioned by Garrison's attorneys, furnish information of a false nature. This would place this Government in a bad position in future criminal proceedings against Walter since this Government probably would have to produce evidence before a court or Federal Grand Jury which it had previously instructed Walter not to furnish under the executive privilege category.
>
> Department feels that we have a prosecutable case at this time under Section 1001, Title 18, U. S. Code, since Walter has furnished conflicting and false data to FBI officials and this Bureau can categorically deny at a court trial or other proceedings that there was a teletype 11/17/63 as alleged by Walter. Department also believes it could subpoena Walter to appear at a Federal Grand Jury where he would be placed under oath. If Walter continues to falsely insist that there was an FBI teletype 11/17/63 reporting threat to President Kennedy, Department could obtain a perjury indictment against Walter.

A portion of the third page of a May 3, 1968, FBI memorandum to W.C. Sullivan, assistant director of the FBI, from W.A. Branigan, chief of the FBI counterespionage section, concerning the assassination of President Kennedy. Showcasing the blatant disparaging of William S. Walter and his story, this memo, in addition to cementing the FBI's all-around negative assessment, also concerns potential ways of "dealing" with Walter's allegation.

Both Sullivan and Branigan retired in the 1970s.

(Public Domain.)

Ja...sville, Florida
February 2, 1968

RE: ASSASSINATION OF PRESIDENT
JOHN FITZGERALD KENNEDY
DALLAS, TEXAS
NOVEMBER 22, 1963

On the morning of February 1, 1968, Mr. WILLIAM
S. WALTER, 1533 Jackson Avenue, New Orleans, Louisiana,
contacted Special Agent in Charge D. K. BROWN by telephone
and furnished the following information:

Mr. WALTER stated he was in Jacksonville for a
short period of time, and on the night of January 31,
1968, he had seen the Johnny Carson Show on television
and that certain representations were made by District
Attorney JIM GARRISON which were inaccurate and untrue.
Mr. WALTER made an appointment to appear at the Jacksonville
Office during the afternoon of February 1, 1968, and furnish
the facts concerning his contacts with people concerned in
the GARRISON investigation of the death of President KENNEDY.

On the afternoon of February 1, 1968, Mr. WALTER
came to the office and advised that the Johnny Carson
Show, supra, consisted of an interview with JIM GARRISON.
Near the end of the show, JOHNNY CARSON was pressing
GARRISON for new evidence he allegedly had to offer and
GARRISON referred to MARK LANE who had been helping
GARRISON in the investigation. GARRISON, according to
Mr. WALTER's recollection, said that MARK/LANE had obtained from Mr. WALTER a sworn statement which reflected that
on the morning of November 17, 1963, Mr. WALTER had received
a "TWX message" directed to all Southern Regional Offices
of the FBI. The message advised that an attempt to assassinate President KENNEDY would be made in Dallas on November 22,

A section of the first page of a memo prepared by the FBI office in Jacksonville, Florida, dated February 2, 1968, which provides a brief chronology of Jim Garrison's appearance on *The Tonight Show* with Johnny Carson. It also, importantly, emphasizes that Walter himself initiated contact with the FBI following Carson's interview with Garrison.

(Public Domain.)

PART TWO: WILLIAM S. WALTER AND THE PHANTOM TELETYPE

Introduction

There are objects in folklore and pop culture that are legendary for many reasons, such as the power they may contain (as with the Ark of the Covenant) or their place at the intersection of theology, history, and culture (as with the fabled Holy Grail). Those are examples of an epic sort, but the same rings true for many items throughout myth and history. The object that this story is concerned with is not powerful, overtly unique, or in any way magical – it is a simple teletype message, which may or may not have been sent; that may or may not have existed in the files of the New Orleans FBI office; that may or may not ever be found.

Tales about mystical or lost objects are never just about the object. In this section of the book, you will meet William S. Walter. His story is much more than a unique assassination anecdote, overlapping with several of the larger components and themes of the overarching narrative (such as the FBI's actions before, during, and after the assassination; Jim Garrison's investigation into the President's murder in New Orleans; and the various reported threats on President Kennedy's life, among others). It is also the story of an individual whose life was in no small way affected by the assassination and by what would normally be just another of the thousands upon thousands of messages sent and received by employees of the federal government.

Walter's story is also notable for how it has seemingly slipped through the cracks, reappearing now and again, but mainly as a footnote to other, sometimes more popular, or more complicated, stories. Walter's experiences connect to the larger picture of the assassination in a bittersweet way – as he was a notably credible witness, and yet, as the above title suggests, the teletype in question was never found. Walter's experiences are also representative of a news establishment that picks and chooses what to report, thereby signaling quickly and assertively which stories matter, and which do not. The stories that get published often help establish what, in the end, becomes "the truth." What chance do the unreported or seldom-reported stories have against something as big as the truth?

William S. Walter's Story

In November of 1963, William S. Walter was one of three security clerks at the Federal Bureau of Investigation (FBI) office in New Orleans, Louisiana. Walter was an FBI employee from June 19, 1961, to August 24, 1966.[xxiii] After resigning from the FBI, he went on to hold positions in various fields, including sales, higher education, and banking.[*] He would eventually become senior vice president

---

[*] A part of Walter's biography was reconstructed using his obituary, published online by Riemann Family Funeral Homes. The obituary notes that Walter's "interest in history, politics and his employment at the New Orleans FBI office at the time of [the] Kennedy assassination led to an ongoing interest in and contact with many of the conspiracy theorist[s] and Warren Report critics." The teletype story clearly had a lasting impact on his life.

108

of Patterson State Bank in Morgan City, Louisiana.[xxiv] Walter has a place in the assassination story for one reason – something he would stand by for decades after the fact: his allegation that, while on overnight duty on November 17, having begun his shift at 12:15 a.m.,[xxv] the New Orleans office received a teletype from FBI headquarters[*] in Washington, D.C., warning of an "attempt to assassinate President Kennedy on his proposed trip to Dallas, Texas, November 22 – 23, 1963."[†]

Over time, specific details like the exact time the teletype was sent and received (keeping in mind the time difference, from Eastern to Central Time), as well as particular FBI teletype formatting, were repeatedly brought up to discredit, or at least weaken, the credibility of Walter's claim. In some ways, one can regard Walter's experience with the alleged teletype like this: a young man who happened to be in the wrong place at the wrong time.[xxvi] Perhaps, if it had not been Walter, on that day, at that time, who happened upon the teletype, then there would never have been anything to look into or debate – there would never have been a "phantom"

---

[*] Walter and his story were briefly depicted in the third act of Oliver Stone's film *JFK*. Although a small component of a much larger plot, the inclusion of Walter's testimony about the warning teletype speaks to the story's importance and resonance.

[†] Incidentally, had President Kennedy not been murdered on November 22, he would have then traveled by motorcade through Austin the following day – "the final destination on President Kennedy's Texas tour" (KUT News, Nov. 22, 2013, Matthew Alvarez).

teletype story. While Walter would become a lone voice among his fellow FBI employees on this subject, this does not automatically detract from the veracity of his allegation and his overall credibility. He would stand by what he saw for the rest of his life.

The New Orleans DA, a Talk Show Host, and an Attorney

New Orleans District Attorney Jim Garrison, who would end up dedicating the rest of his life to investigating the assassination, appeared on *The Tonight Show* with Johnny Carson on January 31, 1968. Garrison hoped to discuss and present some of the findings his office had uncovered in its investigation up to that point on a national scale. Carson's show seemed like a good opportunity to do so. Carson was not as gracious or open toward Garrison as perhaps the District Attorney had expected or wished him to be, but this did not deter Garrison from making his points, answering Carson's questions, and getting some laughs from the audience (Garrison was famous for his dry, but sharp, sense of humor). (This interview can be found on YouTube; it is one of the many examples of the media establishment's attempts at downplaying the seriousness and legitimacy of Garrison's work.)

At one point during the episode, Garrison briefly mentioned Walter and the alleged existence of an FBI teletype that warned of an attempt on the President's life on his fall trip to Texas. Based on internal government memoranda, Walter's testimony before the House Select Subcommittee on Assassinations (HSCA) in 1978, Garrison's own account of the investigation in his book, *On the Trail of the Assassins*, and the detailed work of author Joan Mellen in her book *A Farewell to Justice: Jim Garrison, JFK's Assassination, and the Case That Should Have Changed History*, this author believes that hearing his name mentioned in connection to Garrison's investigation, and the assassination in general, greatly alarmed Walter.[*]

Before Garrison's appearance on *The Tonight Show*, noted Warren Commission critic and attorney Mark Lane and his wife encountered Walter at New Orleans' Tulane University sometime during the first week of December 1967. (Walter attended courses there as a political science and history major and had decided to attend a special presentation by Lane taking place at the college.[xxvii]) Their initial interaction, as well as subsequent attempts on the Lanes' part to convince Walter to divulge anything he might know about the assassination – having recently been employed by the FBI and potentially privy to more information than either of the Lanes – likely contributed to Walter's reluctance in late 1967 and early 1968 to allow himself to be associated with either the potential existence of a warning teletype or the work being conducted at the time by either Lane or Garrison.

Although only mentioned in passing during Garrison's appearance on *The Tonight Show*, Walter – who was in

---

[*] It had been less than two years since Walter had resigned from the FBI, and based on contemporary accounts and memoranda, it is very probable that Walter was worried about some kind of (negative) response from his past employer. It is also likely that, in a more general sense, Walter was concerned about his reputation and his professional future.

Jacksonville, Florida, at the time – contacted the FBI office there and spoke with Special Agent in Charge (SAC) D. K. Brown on February 1, 1968 (this taking place almost immediately after Garrison's appearance on Carson's program[xxviii]). This author believes that Walter reached out to the FBI to put himself in the clear and distance himself from what was, at the time, an especially scandalous proposition: asking questions about the assassination and implying (publicly!) that there could potentially be something afoul at the FBI – or with the federal government in general in relation to the Kennedy assassination.

The internal memo cited above reflects this series of events; it also describes Walter's retelling of his encounter with the Lanes at Tulane, highlighting, based on what Walter shared with SAC Brown, that Mrs. Lane had "rather bluntly stated [to Walter] that 'we have some information indicating that the FBI knew the assassination was going to take place.'" The memo concludes with the following: "Mr. Walter advised that he never received or saw a teletype or other message containing information being sought by Lane." (In reconstructing the chronology of Walter's conversations with the FBI, it became clear how Walter's initial reluctance to work with Mark Lane was taken by the FBI out of context and used to hint that, initially, Walter had been telling the truth to the Lanes, but then had, for some reason, changed his mind and begun lying about the existence of an FBI warning.)

Although their first encounter occurred in part because Walter had attended a presentation by Lane, Walter expressed, in no uncertain terms, that he had no intention of associating himself with either Lane or, for that matter, with any potentially controversial perspectives on the assassination. The same Jacksonville, FBI, memo states that "shortly after this incident [with the Lanes], Mr. Walter left New Orleans to go to Atlanta, where he spent two weeks in a training course for Permacel, the industrial tape division of Johnson and Johnson. He returned to New Orleans the Friday before Christmas, 1967."[xxix] After returning to New Orleans, Lane again attempted to win Walter's cooperation. Lane and a few of his associates apparently tried to convince Walter multiple times to share any knowledge he might possess about the FBI's involvement in either the assassination or the subsequent cover-up. Feeling as though he was being pressured by Lane (and understandably concerned about his future, or any potential problems with the FBI), Walter told Lane that he "had no copies of any Bureau communications and that he knew of no one who did."[xxx]

This basic chronology of events was arrived at using government memoranda, Walter's own first-person accounts, and information collected by Garrison and Mellen in their respective books. It must be noted that while government documents can function as a support device, helping to reconstruct Walter's post-assassination movements, they alone cannot be used to dependably ascertain the reality of Walter's situation. As will be apparent later, some of the FBI memoranda expressed a decidedly adversarial view of Walter and his allegations. As such, it is more than possible that several of these documents were created to editorialize and potentially distort Walter's story.

Lastly, before moving on, it should also be noted that the above episode is not intended to tarnish the work and reputation of Mark Lane, an indisputably courageous and proactive voice among Warren Commission critics. It is this author's opinion, based on extensive research and a variety of sources, that while Walter may have been intimidated by Lane's investigative efforts, his attempts at gaining Walter's trust and learning what information he could were not conducted in any malevolent or irresponsible fashion, or intended to be interpreted as such. In the late 1960s, Lane and Garrison were among the few people in the country willing to publicly challenge the official story and offer alternative evidence and perspectives.

Changing His Story?

It is necessary to note that FBI memoranda outlining Walter's interview with the Jacksonville office of the FBI – and then, a few days later, on February 5, 1968, with SAC Robert Rightmyer of the New Orleans office – underscore that in the early months of that year, Walter had "denied Garrison's allegation."[xxxi] His subsequent meeting with United States Attorney Louis LaCour on March 15, 1968, also in New Orleans, seems to have been a turning point: the moment when Walter *appeared* to have changed his story, informing LaCour "and two of [the] latter's assistants [that] there was such [an] FBI message."[xxxii] When interviewed by the FBI in Tennessee on March 26, Walter stated that, when he had talked with SAC Brown in Jacksonville, "he was not asked whether he actually received the teletype."[xxxiii] This will become an important point for both Walter and the FBI – at which point did either party first explicitly discuss the alleged teletype?

This apparent shift on Walter's part – at first denying the existence of the November 17 teletype, and then saying that there *was* such a document, and that he *had* in fact seen it in New Orleans – would have the FBI, from March 1968 on, repeatedly characterize Walter as someone who positively cannot be trusted. What the FBI did not do, however, is explore the timing of Walter's interviews with the FBI – and what this sequence might mean. Based on the documented information, this author firmly believes that Garrison's mention of Walter and the alleged warning teletype worried, or even alarmed, the former FBI clerk and that he, seeking to distance himself from the controversial Jim Garrison and the persistent Mark Lane, had reached out to the FBI of his own volition – on multiple occasions and in multiple cities while on the road – in an attempt to assuage any concerns the FBI might have about him.

It is curious, also, that the FBI, in the several memos cited throughout, does not once highlight how Walter had initiated his contact with the FBI of his own accord – that he was not once contacted by agents of the Bureau and prompted to appear at a field office to be interviewed.[*]

---

[*] None of the memoranda reviewed for this book state that the FBI sought out Walter in either 1967 or 1968; it was Walter's decision to contact his former employer and to initiate the subsequent interviews.

It is also telling, in a way that supports Walter's character, that while he had received two letters of censure while employed by the FBI – the first on November 20, 1964, "for his failure to properly record several telephonic complaints he received from a woman complainant," and the second, on July 25, 1966, for attending "classes at Tulane University when he was in a sick leave status" – his departure from the Bureau, in August of 1966, was nevertheless voluntary.[xxxiv]

A Liar?

Following his interviews at the Jacksonville and New Orleans FBI field offices where, the agency notes, Walter had denied the existence of a warning teletype, and his meeting with U.S. Attorney LaCour – where, the Bureau reports, Walter's story happened to change – the former FBI clerk would again speak to the agency in Nashville, Tennessee, on March 26, 1968. During this conversation, he "insisted that he *did* receive such a teletype" (emphasis added). According to Walter, when he spoke to the FBI in Nashville, he was apparently asked to sign a statement, which he "refused ... on grounds that [his] attorney was in New Orleans and [he] was in Nashville."[xxxv]

Based on this documented chronology, Walter "changed his story" after meeting with LaCour, at which time Walter's own attorney, Guy Wootan[*] of New Orleans, was also present. While this is admittedly an extrapolation on the

---

[*] Some memoranda spell his last name as "Wootan," while others use "Wooten." It has been difficult to ascertain the correct spelling, but this author believes "Wootan" is the correct spelling.

author's part, one can assume that Walter felt more at ease while in the presence of his attorney and the implicit legal protection that this provided. If this is when Walter began to lie (meaning, as the FBI asserted, that his earlier interviews and denials of the existence of an FBI warning teletype are to be interpreted as the truth) then why would Walter complicate matters for himself by adding certain details to his story – such as what steps he would typically have to follow upon receipt of such a teletype, or how, as part of this procedure, Walter would have to alert the Special Agent in Charge? (Harry Maynor, who had been Walter's SAC, would be added to the ranks of many other New Orleans FBI employees who went on to deny Walter's allegation.)

A May 3, 1968, memorandum from a W.A. Branigan[*] to a W.C. Sullivan[†], while summarizing "certain alternate courses of action the Department [of Justice]" was considering in "dealing with [the] false allegations of William S. Walter" – labeling Walter as "a liar who cannot be trusted" – also recognized that the federal government would be placed in a "bad position in future criminal proceedings against Walter since this Government probably would have to produce evidence before a court or Federal Grand Jury which it had previously instructed Walter not to furnish under the executive privilege category." In attempting to formulate a legal approach that would deal

---

[*] William A. Branigan, Jr. was a specialist in Russian intelligence. He retired as chief of the FBI counterespionage section in 1976.

[†] William Cornelius Sullivan was an assistant director of the FBI, in charge of the agency's domestic intelligence operations from 1961 to 1971.

with Walter's allegation, the FBI was always aware of how its actions against Walter could potentially reflect on the agency. The specific category of "executive privilege" will become an important detail later, particularly within the context of Walter's recollections during his deposition before the HSCA in the mid-1970s.

A Note on Professor Donald E. Wilkes, Jr.

The late law professor Donald E. Wilkes, Jr. spent years writing about the assassination, reviewing contemporary literature on the subject, and publishing pieces that examined both the evidence pertaining to the murder and subsequent investigations, as well as the topic's central, overarching themes. In one 2017 article, published in *Flagpole* Magazine, "Did J. Edgar Hoover Kill JFK?", Wilkes highlights "an obscure Secret Service document dated only two days" prior to the alleged teletype of November 17, 1963. This Secret Service document was first discussed in Vincent Michael Palamara's book, *Survivor's Guilt: The Secret Service and the Failure to Protect President Kennedy*. Wilkes quotes from Palamara's book and summarizes the significance of this document, connecting it to Walter's story.

Found on page 566 in Volume 17 of the *Hearings Before the President's Commission on the Assassination of President Kennedy* (containing the testimony and exhibits referenced within the Warren Report), that Secret Service document, dated November 15, 1963, warned that a "militant group of the National States Rights Party plans to assassinate the President and other high-level officials." This information, per the document, had been "received telephonically from FBI Headquarters, Washington, D.C." The document's existence, its inclusion among the Warren Commission's exhibits, and its temporal proximity to both Walter's alleged teletype and the assassination itself are all factors that – albeit in an indirect manner – serve to substantiate Walter's story. However indirect or not, this obscure document adds to Walter's credibility, particularly when placed in context with his deposition before the HSCA, his statements to Jim Garrison, and his overall credibility as a witness.

(It is frustrating and unfortunate, but not surprising, that the HSCA decided to discredit Walter's deposition in its entirety. A major reason for this decision was the fact that Walter was the only former or current FBI employee to attest to the existence of the November 17 teletype. Nobody else had come forward in all that time.)

The "Phantom Teletype"

Having read the various internal FBI documents and Walter's own complete deposition before the HSCA in 1978, this author agrees with Wilkes, who, in the article cited above, wrote that "Walter's deposition testimony [before the HSCA] was forthright and believable. He had a credible answer to almost every question put to him. He had nothing to gain by testifying." (The warning teletype soon became derisively known as the "phantom teletype," due to the FBI's inability to recover the original copy.) Its details are only known today thanks to Walter's interest in the assassination and his initiative to write down the content of that warning – something that Walter himself speaks to during his 1978 deposition, clarifying that he never stole government property (a physical copy of the teletype), but did paraphrase the content and formatting of the document.

Walter did his best to recount the full chronology of events surrounding the teletype to the HSCA, at the same time making the valid point that his insistence on the matter in no way benefited him – that, in fact, it only encouraged the FBI to accuse Walter of lying. As a byproduct of this, certain researchers and writers ended up casting aside Walter's side of the story altogether. Anthony Summers, in his book *Conspiracy*, wrote briefly about Walter and the teletype, accenting how Walter's credibility had "diminished" by the "unsupported claim, that the FBI learned in advance of a possible threat to the President's life in Dallas."[xxxvi] Other writers have done the same, recounting the allegation of a warning teletype in a few paragraphs or less – to leave no assassination stone unturned, perhaps – only to move on to the larger aspects of the story. Walter's experience, like that of so many others who had found themselves in some way connected to the assassination, helps us to better perceive the massive tides of discreditation, marginalization, and ignorance that so often accompany vast, intricate bureaucracies.

The May 3, 1968, memorandum that characterizes Walter as "a liar who cannot be trusted" would not be the last of its kind. In the same memo, the FBI claims to have "exhaustively reviewed" its records and states that the only Bureau communication "sent to the New Orleans office … from Headquarters" on November 17, 1963, was the "translation of a document completely unrelated to the assassination." The FBI had offered him "Executive Immunity and Executive Privilege if [he] was subpoenaed by Jim Garrison," as Walter explained to the HSCA. He added that, to him, the FBI's "concern seemed ... to be not whether or not what I was saying was fact, but whether or not I was going to cooperate with Garrison in his Clay Shaw trial,* and they offered me legal counsel and were going to advise me on my rights of Executive Privilege." If Executive Privilege had been applied in this case, Walter's side of the story would be legally, and perhaps indefinitely, suppressed.

During his deposition, Walter explained: "If there is anything that has caused me a problem in dealing with the FBI, it has been ... them alleging that I have given conflicting testimony to them concerning what they called the phantom teletype ... I had no ax to grind with the FBI." In his own words, he had "nothing to gain by talking about this." This author agrees.

---

* For about two years, New Orleans District Attorney Jim Garrison and his team worked to prove that local businessman Clay Shaw had prior knowledge of President Kennedy's assassination; had contact with Lee Harvey Oswald, among others, prior to the assassination; and had CIA connections. While Garrison and his team lost the trial, years later, it was discovered that Shaw, in fact, *had* ties to the CIA. The passage of time and the work of researchers have also proven that the CIA and FBI both had a vested interest in stopping and discrediting Garrison's investigation. The case and all its players are covered in the exceptional book *A Farewell to Justice* by Joan Mellen.

The Only One?

In addition to Walter, two other security patrol clerks were working at the New Orleans FBI office at the time: Thomas Cecil McCurley and Thomas J. Bevans. They went on the record as denying any knowledge of a warning teletype.[xxxvii] The FBI went to the trouble of interviewing 53 other employees, all of whom "denied any knowledge of the receipt of any teletype or other type of communication on November 17, 1963, containing information that there might be an assassination attempt on President Kennedy in Texas." These 53 individuals also stated that neither Walter "nor anyone else had contacted them in an effort to determine whether such a communication exists."[xxxviii] (Harry G. Maynor, who had been the Special Agent in Charge of the New Orleans FBI office when Walter was employed there, was interviewed in March of 1968 and stated that he had "no recollection whatever of receiving or seeing any such teletype or other communication containing a message that there would be a threat to President Kennedy in connection with the latter's trip to Texas."[xxxix] Maynor also stated that "had such a message been received, he most certainly would have had some recollection of it.")

While the FBI did its due diligence – developing a list of employees who flatly denied Walter's claim and declaring, officially, that after a thorough search of its records, no such teletype, dating to or around November 17, 1963, could be found – Walter's story, from the mid-1960s well into the late 70s, as well as his candor before the HSCA and the general consistency of his story, all point to a profoundly disheartening narrative: that of a young, former, lower-level FBI employee and U.S. citizen whose story was discredited at almost every turn by a system that, in theory, is meant to work *for* the people and not against them. If it had not been for Garrison's brief passage about Walter and the teletype in his book *On the Trail of the Assassins*, for Joan Mellen's highly-detailed reporting of Walter's story and of his eventual acquaintance with Garrison, or for Ray and Mary LaFontaine's book, *Oswald Talked*, the "phantom teletype" would likely not have amounted to the kind of story that it does today. These books, written at different times and by vastly different people, helped support Walter's credibility and recontextualize the "phantom teletype" as an important piece of the larger puzzle.

The original document – or even a copy of it – was never recovered, and likely never will be. Even so, great significance can be found in both the physical absence of the teletype and the metaphorical absence of any kind of resolution to this story. It would, of course, be wonderful if this part of Walter's HSCA testimony could somehow, one day, become a reality: "One day it is going to come out that the teletype did exist."[xl]

Lee Harvey Oswald, Informant?

In addition to the lengthy chronology of the alleged "phantom teletype" – to include the implications arising from the FBI's response to Walter; how Walter was characterized in internal memoranda; and the overall consistency of his story across the span of decades – there is also the matter of another allegation brought up by Walter during his deposition before the House Select Committee on Assassinations... Walter testified that in response to a request for a file check, he had found "both a security and an informant file on Oswald" in the files of the FBI in New Orleans.[xli] Speculation surrounding Lee Harvey Oswald's possible connections to either the FBI or CIA (or both) has persisted for a long time. While Walter's FBI teletype never materialized, his testimony regarding Oswald's "security and ... informant file" is not only very credible but severely damning – as the agency spent a long time denying any and all ties to Oswald. Because neither allegation could be substantiated by the HSCA, and because various testimonies by FBI personnel countered Walter's claims about the teletype and Lee Harvey Oswald's possible role as an FBI informant, the HSCA, in its final report[*], decided that Walter was not worth trusting, writing simply that they were "led to question Walter's credibility."[xlii]

James Hosty, FBI

During his deposition before the Subcommittee on Civil and Constitutional Rights on December 12, 1975 (a Congressional body that, at the time, was holding hearings on the subject of FBI oversight) FBI Special Agent James

---

[*] In their book *Oswald Talked*, Ray and Mary LaFontaine note in the preface that Walter's deposition before the HSCA was not released until 1993, "by which time it had become obvious that HSCA counsel Robert Blakey distorted the testimony in the HSCA's Report issued in 1979." Whatever distortions occurred or were implemented, delaying the release of Walter's testimony does not put the HSCA in a favorable light.

Hosty was asked by California Representative Don Edwards if Hosty had "any knowledge of an alleged Telex (another word for teletype) that was received in all Southern field offices shortly before the assassination warning that President Kennedy might be assassinated in Dallas."[xliii] Hosty was present before the Subcommittee for an entirely different reason,[*] but nonetheless answered the question in the same way he answered all others put to him – in a straightforward, professional matter: "I was questioned about that the last few months, the same as many agents around the FBI were, and if any such teletype existed, it would have been brought to my attention." He added that, "I feel that this person is referring to a teletype that was sent after the assassination of President Kennedy and before the identification of Lee Oswald as the assassin."[xliv]

During his 1978 deposition before the House Select Committee on Assassinations, HSCA staff counsel Robert W. Genzman asked Walter if the New Orleans FBI office received a teletype "on the afternoon of November 22, 1963." Walter replied: "I now know that either on the afternoon of the assassination or the night of the

---

[*] Hosty, and other members of the FBI and employees of the Dallas, Texas office, had been called to testify about the matter of a letter that Oswald delivered to the Dallas office ten days before the assassination (*The New York Times*, September 17, 1975). In short, agent Hosty was ordered to destroy the letter by Dallas SAC J. Gordon Shanklin. As with many other aspects of the assassination, there has been debate over the content and significance of the Oswald note, as well as the issue of how the FBI dealt with this letter. "Some time later, Mr. Hoover sent out letters of censure to 17 agents and F.B.I. officials because of the incident, and Mr. Hosty was suspended without pay for 30 days and transferred to … Kansas City" (Ibid).

assassination the Washington field office or the Director sent a teletype to all field offices advising them to contact their informants to determine what information might be developed on a possible plot that caused the death of President Kennedy."[xlv]

Genzman then asked: "Mr. Walter, is it at all possible that you could be confusing this November 22nd teletype with the teletype which you claimed to have received on November 17, 1963?"

Walter, remaining firm, replied: "They are very similar in wording and context, but in light of what went through my head and what discussions took place immediately after the assassination, there is no possible way for me to be confusing the two teletypes."[xlvi]

A part of the FBI's argument against the validity of Walter's allegation was the apparent inconsistency in formatting that Walter recounted. (He never kept a physical copy of the teletype, not wanting to break the law and jeopardize his employment with the FBI, relying instead on a hand-written, then typed, copy, as well as his memory.)

The question of where the warning teletype of November 17, 1963, was sent is perhaps more interesting than it is important, but it is yet another point of contention in this narrative. Hosty testified that he had heard of a teletype that was "received in all Southern field offices," but other sources state that it was received nationwide, by all field offices across the country. This was, in fact, never fully answered. Garrison, in his book, writes that the teletype was "addressed to all special agents in charge, which meant everyone in the country."[xlvii] In its internal memoranda, the FBI notes that if indeed the teletype had been addressed to every SAC in the country, then surely Walter must be lying. How can 50-plus other FBI personnel be wrong and Walter – the sole (former) FBI employee – be right? This supposed discrepancy —some saying the teletype was sent nationwide, others that it was sent only to the SACs in the southwest —was one of the several points used against Walter throughout the ordeal.

Notes On A Deposition

William S. Walter's deposition before the House Select Committee on Assassinations on March 23, 1978, was provided before HSCA Staff Counsel Robert W. Genzman, Senior Staff Counsel Michael Goldsmith, Deputy Chief Counsel Gary Cornwall, and Notary Elizabeth Berning. During the deposition, Walter stated that he found it "very difficult to talk about the things that came into my knowledge during my tenure with the FBI in that it would place some unfavorable light on the Bureau. How this came about, that I got involved with talking about anything with the FBI is disappointing to me, but it did happen." He goes on to note that "it happened in 1968 [when Jim Garrison appeared on *The Tonight Show*], when, I might add, it was not very popular to talk about government confidential information and, personally, I was not in a position to take on the Bureau if I had wanted to."[xlviii]

While his deposition was essentially ignored and, within the confines of the HSCA's Report, his credibility tarnished, Walter does speak candidly and thoughtfully, sharing personal details that add further context and believability to his core allegation – that there *had* been a warning teletype received at the New Orleans office. "I did not have any money. I just got a new job. I was involved with a divorce. I was out in an area away from home, and the last thing I needed was any publicity [potentially as a result of Garrison's interview with Johnny Carson], any conflict with the Bureau and any dealings with anybody with the Bureau."[xlix] Walter further stressed that his "only purpose in being in that office [the Jacksonville, Florida, FBI office] was to be certain that the FBI knew that in no way did [he] divulge any confidential information."[l]

Walter's testimony is doubly interesting for the historical context it alludes to. His testimony was given before a legislative body in the recent aftermath of the Watergate scandal which was, for the time, a very shocking, seismic, event that culminated in President Nixon's resignation.[*] Walter explained to HSCA counsel that he "watched and read [about] Watergate,[†] and [he] saw and heard of things

---

[*] Nixon resigned in 1974.

[†] Following the original news coverage in the *Washington Post* by Bob Woodward and Carl Bernstein, the two told their story in a book, *All the President's Men*. In 1976, that book was made into a movie of the same name. When saying that he "watched and read [about] Watergate," Walter was likely referring to the seminal film, as well as perhaps related developments on TV news.

that happened in the Bureau."[li] He continued: "I tend to, on the surface, think that it is impossible for a teletype to be received and sent on that date [November 17, 1963] concerning a killing of a very popular President and that that information does not somehow get out. *I have doubted myself from time to time over the past 14 years*, but I can still recall that [sic] the actual things that I did to that document, with that document, and the conversations that I had with people and the feeling that I had on the morning of the 22nd, to know that I am not mistaken."[lii] (Emphasis added.)

Speaking about the 53 FBI employees that were interviewed about the teletype – all denying the existence of such a document – Walter explained that it was not "a very popular thing in 1968 for these people to know anything about a teletype that was sent, received, or had anything to do with embarrassing the Bureau, especially present Bureau employees … I just don't think, when Mr. Hoover* was alive in 1968, that these individuals wanted to stand up and say anything about the assassination investigation."[liii] Walter

---

* J. Edgar Hoover had led the FBI for 48 years. A multifaceted character, a pioneering lawman and a master of self-promotion and image-building, Hoover was in no small part responsible for the iconic "G Man" aesthetic of the clean-cut, hard-on-crime FBI operative. A difficult individual, both personally and professionally, he has been the subject of many books, as well as a film directed by Clint Eastwood and starring Leonardo DiCaprio. His nearly 50 years of service as FBI Director are nothing short of a legacy that is, in many ways, still with us. Complex and contradictory, his iron-fisted influence over the many facets of day-to-day FBI operations persisted long after his death in 1972.

never kept a copy of the teletype because, in his mind, that would have been both dishonest and against the rules and policies set forth by the FBI, his employer at the time. As Garrison writes on page 221 of his book, *On the Trail of the Assassins*, "at the time [Walter] copied the exact phraseology of the telex* warning and kept it." Ultimately, Walter's story about the "phantom teletype," as revealed in memoranda and books, rarely touches on the *possession* of a government document. The real question has always been whether it had existed at all.

For decades, the FBI maintained that the teletype never existed. Garrison, going off Walter's own words, writes that "shortly afterwards [November 17, Walter] checked the file again to see if the warning was still there. It had been removed." During his deposition, Walter explained: "My only intention with that document was to use it for my own information, and I was only interested in the context of the meat of the teletype."[liv] Senior Staff Counsel Goldsmith then asked Walter: "Why didn't you Xerox it?" Walter replied that he "didn't want to have a copy of that teletype in my briefcase or any other government documents. I was concerned about my oath to the position that I held."[lv]

Walter continued, saying: "I want the committee to know that I have no reason to want to lie about this kind of thing. I am perfectly confident that everything I told the committee is accurate, even though I was somewhat not prepared to be

---

* The word teletype or telex can be, and often are, used interchangeably. For the sake of cohesion, this author has been using "teletype."

questioned today, and have many, many more busy things
that I have occupied my time with in the past 14 years. I
know it is going to be difficult for anybody to come forward
at this late date and acknowledge that there was such a
teletype, and I doubt that it will be done any time in the
future – in the near future."[lvi]

Following Up

An "informative note" developed by the Domestic
Intelligence Division of the FBI, dated March 22, 1968,
summarized the "phantom teletype" situation thusly:
"William Walter is a former security patrol clerk of the New
Orleans Office, who has changed his story repeatedly
concerning an alleged FBI message sent to New Orleans
11/17/63, reporting a threat against President Kennedy.
There was no such communication. The New Orleans Office
has been instructed to interview Walter, pin down his story,
and obtain a signed statement ... We are following this
matter closely."[lvii] The matter *was* followed. Over the
subsequent years, the FBI would keep tabs on both Walter
and this pesky matter of the "phantom teletype."

An FBI memorandum dated September 30, 1975, concerns
Louis Ann Nolan, an FBI clerk who had been
"telephonically contacted ... by Ed Clancey, Radio Station
WGSO (New Orleans, Louisiana)" about the FBI document.
The memo stresses that "Miss Nolan advised Clancey that
she had not seen such a communication (the warning
teletype of November 17, 1963)."[lviii] This same memo details
a telephone conversation between Barry Sussman of the
Washington Post and the former SAC of the FBI office in

New Orleans, Harry Maynor, concerning William Walter and the teletype. The call took place on the evening of the previous day. Maynor had "advised Suffman [sic] that he could not confirm the existence of such a teletype because there never was such a teletype."

The story of an alleged FBI teletype warning about a potential threat to President Kennedy's life in Dallas was featured on CBS *Evening News* on September 30, 1975. The story opened with a quick report on Mark Lane and his assertion that the FBI had known five days "in advance of the attempt to kill President John F. Kennedy."[lix] At the time, Lane was director of the Citizens' Commission of Inquiry, leading their campaign to reopen the investigation into the assassination. The CBS report added that Lane's charges were based on "information from ex-FBI security clerk, William Walter." Summarizing the situation, the report explained that Walter, in his role as FBI "overnight code clerk," had received a teletype in the early morning hours of November 17, 1963, warning of an "assassination attempt to be made on Kennedy on November 22" in Dallas, Texas. "FBI director Clarence Kelley says [there is] no evidence to support Walter's allegation or indicate plausibility. [He] says [that a] check of [the] files showed no such teletype."[lx]

On October 1 of that year (about two years prior to his deposition before the House Select Committee on Assassinations), Walter taped an interview[*] with WGSO

---

[*] The quotes presented here from the radio interview are taken from an FBI transcript made of the conversation between Walter and the WGSO interviewer. There are several typos in the transcript

Radio in New Orleans and dutifully explained his side of the story. Asked by the WGSO interviewer, "Well, the FBI here is is [sic] denying any sort of knowledge of that memo or any kind of teletype message whatsoever. Are they just mistaken, or lying or covering up, or what?"[lxi] Walter replied with the following:

"Well, that, you know that's, well, I guess that's for the public to decide. I'm willing to go to a Grand Jury or a Senate investigative hearing and give and give [sic] the evidence that I have and also name names and I think possibly the Bureau has always taken the position, and I don't have anything against the Bureau. I worked there for five and a half years. Er, [sic] the Bureau's always taken the position of don't embarrass the Bureau and they felt at this time that this information couldn't couldn't [sic] have been handled in a more professional manner and wouldn't have had any er, effect at all on who would assassinate Kennedy or of the outcome of the assassination."

While Walter stood by his allegation of a warning teletype, he did not use the opportunities afforded to him to share his story with a wider audience, to also lambast the FBI, or to outrightly claim any conscious malfeasance on the agency's part. And, as in other times he had been interviewed or deposed, Walter also told WGSO that he was "convinced that Oswald was the lone assassin." Unlike many individuals whose stories and personal experiences contested with what

that have been preserved here in an attempt to be as straightforward and direct as possible in relation to the usage of all materials, either quoted or reproduced, throughout this book.

the official opinion may have been, it is clear that Walter was not intent on criticizing the FBI or on proving in any way that Oswald was not the assassin. His concern, simply, had to do with a government message that he says was received by a satellite office of the FBI — the physical trace of which ended up vanishing and its very existence being wholly denied.

Utterly Impossible?

Starting on page 24 of his HSCA deposition, Walter – speaking to Robert Genzman, Staff Counsel – explains that the warning teletype did not mean "a lot" to him then. "It was only after the assassination on the 22nd that that became an important document mainly because it was an embarrassing document." He continues: "I, at that time, was a full-time student at Tulane University, in Political Science, had an interest in history, was a Kennedy fan, and felt that I wanted to use the spare time that I had at the FBI office to track the investigation. So that, if I felt that the Warren Commission did not completely make known to the public the entire circumstances around the FBI's involvement in the investigation, that I could then go to Representative [Hale] Boggs, who was from New Orleans, who I had met on a couple of occasions, and ask him specifically why they weren't included." The explanation Walter offered the HSCA as to why he ever got involved with the November 17 teletype in the first place has been one of the many consistent aspects of his story.

Hale Boggs was, of course, one of the seven leading members of the Warren Commission. A Congressional

Representative from New Orleans, Louisiana, representing the Democratic Party, he was House Majority Leader until his untimely death on or about October 16, 1972, when he, along with Alaska Representative Nicholas Begich, an aide working for Begich, and their pilot, disappeared somewhere between Anchorage and Juneau in a chartered twin-engine Cessna. Boggs had been campaigning in support of Begich, stopping in Anchorage on October 15. Their next stop would have been Juneau, Alaska's state capital.[lxii] The Boggs disappearance resulted in "the largest search and rescue operation to that point in American history, involving 40 military aircraft, 50 civilian planes, a search grid of 325,000 square miles, and more than 3,600 hours of search time." 39 days had passed, and the search was called off. There was no sign of either the wreckage or any survivors.[lxiii]

Boggs was unique among his fellow commissioners. He was perhaps closest in sentiment to Senator Richard Russell and, unlike Gerald Ford, for example, was not always keen on letting "sleeping dogs lie." During an executive session of the Commission on January 27, 1964, Boggs and Allen Dulles had an exchange that colored the majority of the proceedings and the Commission's final results. Having been asked if it were possible to disprove whether someone was an agent of the U.S. clandestine services, Dulles replied to Boggs that he "never knew how to disprove it." Despite Boggs' sensible prodding, the conversation essentially boiled down to this: Dulles, a spymaster with experience dating back to the Second World War, explained that even under oath, it would not be possible to prove or disprove whether someone was then, or had been in the past, a secret operative.

Boggs remarked to Dulles: "…What you do is … Make our problem utterly impossible because you say this rumor [that Oswald may have been an FBI informant] can't be dissipated under any circumstances."[lxiv] Dulles was content to leave it at that.

PART THREE: A PLACE IN HISTORY

"A quarter century later, it is possible to see that the assassination and cover-up by the government and the media were watershed events for this country. They represented the loss of innocence for post-war Americans, the beginning of the current era of discontent and distrust in our government and our most fundamental institutions."

– Jim Garrison, *On the Trail of the Assassins.*

Too Much Time?

Some, even those who disagreed with the Warren Commission and its Report – such as lawyer and critic Vincent Salandria – have pointed out the apparent futility of continuing any kind of re-investigation into the assassination of President Kennedy. "'All the critics, myself included, were misled very early … We spent too much time and effort microanalyzing the details … when all the time it was obvious … that it was a conspiracy.'"[lxv]

"'We must … not waste any more time microanalyzing … That's exactly what they want us to do.'" There is truth to this. A lot of time *has* passed – perhaps too much time. And as far as microanalyzing goes, maybe this author's year-long focus on Walter's story was, in itself, an ultimately hollow exercise, a waste of time. On the other hand, it can be beneficial to have the time and distance to grasp the size and dimensions of a problem, to evaluate and reevaluate its intricacies, and discover the best interpretation or approach.

Memories fade. Pieces of information and evidence can be lost or destroyed (and in many cases, that is exactly what happened). But amid all this erosion, a counter-narrative persists, driven by a desire to seek out and preserve the truth, whatever that truth may be. If nothing else, Walter's story is a modest example of this kind of endeavor. In the final analysis, it is very human to be stubborn about something, to persist until a solution is found. Even if an answer never comes, it is that persistent nagging and scouring that matter.

There are many who still care and many others who, at some point or another, will start to care. Maybe the best approach now for those interested in or even a little curious about the real truth, and not the presented truth, about the assassination of President Kennedy, is to learn how to recognize efforts at misdirection and deception as they happen, whatever the forum or medium. When November 22 rolls around again, try to keep an eye out for the articles, think-pieces, and other content that will undoubtedly be released in commemoration of the assassination. Has anything changed? Has the field widened? Or is Lee Harvey Oswald still the sole culprit?

There are many theories about just how involved agencies of the federal government were in the assassination. There are countless examples of different agencies, in addition to the news media, either suppressing, destroying, or mischaracterizing the facts. Now, in 2025, the real problem is this: those who consider 60-plus years of work and dedication to the truth an inherently worthless and misguided effort. *Why can't people just accept that Oswald did it? Why can't some people just move on?* It seems that many *have* moved on. The news media have, in many ways, helped them do just that. The hearts and minds of millions of Americans are still swayed by the traditional news media. For those who are fine with what they get – the notion that it was a crazed, lone assassin – why should these people be disheartened with what they read in their newspapers and magazines?

The American press, as an institution and an industry, is a crucial component of our unique democratic experiment. Not as powerful as the FBI or CIA, but pervasive, influential, powerful, and entrenched in our vibrant culture. Like any human endeavor, it is full of errors and fallacies, but journalism and the press are not just parts of the American democratic whole – they are often the building blocks of change and progress. Think of some of the most iconic headlines or front pages from the past 100 years – many of them did not just recount the news, but helped transform how people saw the world, their country, and each other.

Having explored the shifts in media processes and consumption from the mid-1960s to the present, it is difficult to ignore or sidestep the many egregious behaviors and practices that have become the norm: excessive polarization, fear mongering, and the overwhelming influence of big business, which has led to an unwarranted and dangerous commodification of the news.

Journalism, at its core, is a practice that works best when it works for all people, helping keep everyone informed and aware as active participants in their democracy, communities, and personal lives. This works best without cherry-picking one's sponsors or giving special treatment to some while leaving others out of a story in which they deserve to be heard. Economic survival is vital for the longevity of any business enterprise, but there is a reason why journalism is enshrined in the First Amendment. It is a special calling and a unique vocation.

The news media today exists as a dizzying series of revolving doors. News outlets today must vie for people's time and attention just as the entertainment industry does. This has transformed how stories are constructed and presented, whether in print or on the screen, with a near-constant emphasis on attention-grabbing content and presentation. However, this is how the situation stands *today*. Neither the news media nor our democracy exists as static objects; they are processes built around fundamental human aspirations and are subject to change – by design. American history, too, is in a continual state of development.

There are countless stories and countless authors, adding and subtracting according to the desires and demands of the time. Perhaps, as more time passes, an emphasis on fact and fairness may yet dominate American journalism. Maybe, somehow, independent news creators, such as those who make YouTube videos, will one day form a union that supersedes the empire presided over by traditional news media corporations and conglomerates – but who knows? For now, let us focus on what the individual can do. And yes, while one individual's media literacy skills may not seem like a powerful enough solution at the moment, it is a skill worth pursuing—and helping others pursue as well. The news media work for us, the people, but it is up to us not to passively take in what we are given; to actively pursue and understand the news and how it is made.

Truth and Power

This book began with an overview and analysis of the American news media: how people used to consume it; how they do so today; and how the assassination and the work of those who disagree with the official verdict have been continually mischaracterized and misrepresented by the news media. The cumulative effect has not been positive, and unfortunately, this is unlikely to change any time soon.

William S. Walter, his story and experiences in connection to President Kennedy's assassination, are at this book's literal and thematic center. Scathing FBI memos deride Walter, citing his apparent unreliability, and branding him a liar, this former employee of the Bureau who, decades after the fact and during his deposition before the HSCA, would point out that he had "nothing to gain by talking" about that so-called "phantom" teletype and that he "had no ax to grind with the FBI." Outside of what the FBI had to say about him, Walter's story – spanning decades – has found its way into notable books on the assassination, such as Jim Garrison's *On the Trail of the Assassins*, Joan Mellen's *A Farewell to Justice*, Ray and Mary LaFontaine's *Oswald Talked*, Jim Marrs' *Crossfire*, and Henry Hurt's *Reasonable Doubt*, as well as articles and book reviews, particularly the efforts of the late professor Donald E. Wilkes, Jr.

In his televised response to an NBC report about his investigation into the assassination, Jim Garrison plainly stated that "there is no room in America for thought control of any kind, no matter how benevolent the objective." All those years ago, Garrison proclaimed: "the day has not yet arrived when the only reality is power and the ideals on which our country was built are merely words printed on paper. I believe that those news agencies which have sought to imply that I would use improper methods to gain some sort of fictional political advantage have simply revealed their own cynicism. I believe that in this conflict between truth and power ... that power cannot possibly smash truth out of existence. The people in this country will not let that happen."

This author looks back on Garrison's televised presentation, considers his words, and hopes against hope that, in the end, truth will ultimately triumph, usurping the power of the mainstream news agencies and the federal government to orchestrate rather than showcase the facts, and finally setting the record straight. However long it takes, it will be up to individual Americans to undo 60-plus years of inaccuracies and lies surrounding the assassination of our President. To echo Garrison's remarks, America is still a nation in which the people make the decisions – whether that is through the ballot box or by the simple, common-sense discernment of facts presented to them by their news media. This book is a small contribution to that process.

New JFK Assassination Documents, January – March, 2025

In January of this year, an executive order was signed to release the remainder of the classified government documents pertaining to the assassinations of John F. Kennedy, Dr. Martin Luther King, Jr., and Robert F. Kennedy. This garnered some headlines and a CNN interview with longtime Warren Commission defender Gerald Posner. Shortly thereafter, in late March – early April, it was reported that the rest of the documents had finally been released. Oliver Stone, the director of *JFK*, had traveled to Congress to testify, urging the nation's legislative branch to reopen the investigation. Even a cursory review of the articles published about Stone's testimony reveals a deliberate disinterest in pursuing the facts and evidence contrary to that of the official conclusion. It is likely that following the initial brouhaha of Stone's testimony, the subject will once again be put on pause at least until the assassination's anniversary date.

It will take time for researchers to parse through this mixed blessing. Sixty-plus years have passed. Documents and evidence can always be – and on occasion, have been – lost, altered, or simply destroyed. Less dramatically, released documents are not always going to reach someone in a legible, easy-to-understand, or even easy-to-read format. A final answer, some ultimate truth about President Kennedy's violent death, will not be found in any official government record. Speaking with author and researcher J. Gary Shaw, about the efficacy of relying on declassified documents to reach the truth, he stated simply that, "You're not going to find anything in the documents that you can hang your hat on."

After discussing the new documents with Henry Hurt, this author agrees that these new files may provide more context or useful background information, but in the end, they will only support what researchers have already known for years. To echo Vincent Salandria's words, "all the time it was obvious … that it was a conspiracy." There may very well be some new leads to follow up on, or something of interest that had been neglected or overlooked (one enticing nugget, as reported by MSNBC on March 18, 2025, is further, unmistakable corroboration concerning Lee Harvey Oswald's links to the CIA), but, the final answer is not among those documents, and perhaps it never was, anyway. If anything, the most revealing aspect of this months-long episode is not the documents themselves – or some final, shocking, revealing piece of information within them – but how the news media has continued to uphold its overall irresponsible, unprofessional, and damaging attitude toward the assassination.

A USA Today article published on March 18, 2025, states that "nothing in the documents has changed the long-held findings that Lee Harvey Oswald acted alone in assassinating Kennedy on Nov. 22, 1963." Another article, published by ABC News on April 1, 2025, covering Stone's Congressional testimony, had this to say: "The newly declassified versions of these documents did not substantively change what is known about the central

Warren Commission finding that Stone has called into question: that Oswald was the lone gunman."

This is a grossly reductive view of six decades of evidence to the contrary, expressed by two of the nation's largest, mainstream news organizations. As a researcher and former journalist, it is confounding, even maddening, to witness this kind of reporting carried out by long-standing and respected news organizations like these. Perhaps what we are seeing is an inversion of Dr. Crenshaw's "conspiracy of silence." This is not silent, but right in our face; a conspiracy of deliberate, obdurate misinformation. With the veritable Mount Everest of existing evidence in mind, Shaw told this author that "You don't have to try to find anything more to prove that Oswald is innocent." It is a shame that many of today's journalists see this differently.

What History Can Make Of Us

"The Pentagon Papers, the My Lai Massacre – these were stories of lasting significance. They showed that all was not as it seemed, that the history we had been taught was full of lies … This was the journalism that showed why freedom of the press was so sacred that it was codified in the First Amendment to the Constitution."

– Craig Unger, *Den of Spies: Reagan, Carter, and the Secret History of the Treason That Stole the White House.*

America and Americans are many things. It is a unique country, a special democratic experiment, turning 250 years old in 2026. Compared to other nations, America and

Americans have experienced and lived through a great deal in just over 200 years, including massive shifts in power, government, and culture. Many of these shifts were inherently good and just—such as the abolition of slavery; the Civil Rights Act and the Voting Rights Act of the 1960s; NASA's efforts in space exploration; and life-changing advancements in medicine and vaccines… It is a long list.

Another quality that makes America unique? It is a massive melting pot of cultures, people, religions, and ideologies that, by and large, have a vested interest in a core tenet of the Declaration of Independence: "Life, liberty, and the pursuit of happiness." Ours is far from a perfect or even consistent track record, but there is much in America's history that continues to give this author, and others, hope. Another point: human beings have a natural instinct for the truth. When the facts are not readily apparent, imagination will work overtime to patch up any remaining discrepancies. However, the "conspiracy theorists" in this case were never the ones responsible for the holes in the larger narrative or for the inconsistencies and confusion inherent in the official story.

Because a president was murdered in cold blood, and the truth, time and again, has been thoroughly mishandled, and because this president represented a new beginning, a new America that would respond to and support a greater variety of people than it had before, an America that would bravely move toward the future, not backward into the past, people have continued to care. To some extent, President Kennedy's remarkable legacy has spurred people to discover and confront the injustice at the heart of his murder and at the core of the resulting cover-up.[*]

Garrison's Lasting Impact

In addition to his work investigating the New Orleans connection to President Kennedy's assassination, Garrison took up involvement in the case in other ways, sticking to his suspicions long after Shaw's acquittal. Despite criticism directed at Garrison from the news establishment, as well as some assassination authors and researchers – such as Patricia Lambert, author of *False Witness: The Real Story of Jim Garrison's Investigation and Oliver Stone's Film JFK*, and Gerald Posner, author of *Case Closed: Lee Harvey Oswald and the Assassination of JFK* – Garrison was, and still is, an important figure among Warren Commission critics. He was among the first to gain national attention for his work, for displaying previously locked-away evidence, and, most importantly, he never backed down.

Part of the criticism lodged against Garrison dealt with his well-documented use of television and reporters. In fact, Garrison, who won his first campaign for District Attorney of New Orleans as an Independent, conducted his campaign largely via televised appearances. His direct, yet personable

---

[*] "Cover-up," in this sense, is not meant to be understood as one overarching, multifaceted conspiracy coordinated by a single source. In fact, as many researchers have shown, several distinct but related cover-up activities were taking place. Sometimes, these actions were as simple as one agency withholding evidence from another; sometimes, the reasons were not grand schemes but simple cowardice, or fear of ridicule and retribution.

manner became something of a trademark. In his meticulously researched, even-handed tome on the assassination, *Reasonable Doubt*, Henry Hurt shares some of his misgivings about Garrison's handling of the case against Shaw – but he also acknowledges Garrison's contribution to history: the prosecution's presentation of the Zapruder film in court marked the first time it was shown to members of the general public.

Writing two books about the assassination (prior to *On the Trail of the Assassins*, he penned *Heritage of Stone*), Garrison continued to speak out publicly in defense of his theory: that elements of the CIA and the Pentagon, along with some anti-Castro Cubans, had conspired to plan and carry out the assassination of President Kennedy – with Oswald as the designated "patsy," or "fall guy." Garrison's theory, detailed in the film *JFK*, maintains that part of the motive for the assassination was the survival and perpetuation of the U.S. military-industrial complex, a concept in geopolitics and economics, but also a functioning process. (An idea that President Dwight D. Eisenhower warned Americans of in his televised farewell address.) Garrison would consistently stand by his theory and convictions, contextualizing the assassination of President Kennedy as a coup d'état.

Writing about the post-assassination period and the cultural climate at the time, Garrison notes in *A Heritage of Stone* that "our military, intelligence agencies, anti-Communist politicians and the media would not have hesitated to raise the possibility of Communist involvement had there been the

148

slightest chance of Communist intelligence present in Dealey Plaza. Why, then, was there such immobilization of our government after the assassination? Action was called for, but the government would not act except when there was opportunity to implicate Lee Oswald, and here, invariably, the government overreacted."[lxvi]

Elaborating on what he perceived as a kind of political and cultural fallout resulting from President Kennedy's murder, Garrison writes that "the assassination reduced the President of the United States to a transient official, a servant of the warfare conglomerate. His assignment is to speak as often as possible about the nation's desire for peace, while he serves as a business agent in Congress for the military and their hardware manufacturers."[lxvii]

Speaking about what he perceived as an "unbroken silence" from the corridors of American power, Garrison wrote: "It is inconceivable that men high in our government today are not fully aware of what really happened to John Kennedy and why it happened. If it can be understood outside Washington, it can be understood in Washington. Yet their sophisticated silence remains unbroken as they continue to play the game that all is well in America."[lxviii]

While that official silence is not as complete or powerful as it was in the days when the Warren Report was the final word on the matter, some of it persists. Garrison noted, all the way back in 1970, that the "sophisticated silence remains unbroken." Perhaps it is that element of sophistication that perpetuates it. The abstinence from the total truth about the assassination is carried out in several ways, large and small. Sometimes it is the destruction of evidence, at other times, the steady stream of denials and half-truths. Yet in other situations, it is a non-denial denial —a skirting away that is special because of *how* people stay quiet, *how* questions remain unanswered. The delay continues.

A Worthy Comparison

Unlike "Watergate," for example – a scandal that incontrovertibly affected the country and represented another major shift in American culture towards a strong dissatisfaction in and distrust of the nation's institutions – the assassination of President Kennedy is not a finite topic. Watergate happened. President Richard Nixon's criminal acts were investigated, reported on, and exposed, and he became the first president in American history to resign from his post. President Gerald Ford's pardoning of Nixon sent shockwaves through the culture but possibly helped keep the country from splitting apart in the end. In any case, the key players are well known; the questions have answers. People today can have a heated debate about Nixon's policies and decisions, but very few can argue about Watergate itself and Nixon's role in it. When it comes to the assassination, however, this is not the case. Both events can be seen as separate aspects of the American story, as well as historical events that were both of their time and helped define it. But President Kennedy's assassination goes beyond the constraints that Nixon and Watergate inhabit; the assassination has, for better or worse, evolved into lore.

This is a testament to the importance that the assassination has held in the minds and imaginations of millions of Americans. Likewise, Watergate has persisted as a fascinating tale of political intrigue and a symbol of pervasive corruption and cynicism; however, the glaring holes have been filled, and significant questions have been answered. Furthermore, Watergate affected civil servants, politicians, journalists, and even members of the intelligence community; there is no doubt about this. Watergate can rightfully be seen as the death of post-WWII American naïveté. The death of President Kennedy, on the other hand, still lingers – spectral and supernatural by comparison to the grounded, dry realities of taped conversations, illicit funds, and office break-ins.

Following The Money

With Watergate in mind, this author briefly entertained the idea of "following the money." (In the film, *All the President's Men*, "Deep Throat," played by Hal Holbrook, suggests that Robert Redford's Bob Woodward should "follow the money" – that by tracking the shadowy financial patterns that surrounded the overall mystery, he would be able to penetrate its secrets.) In the time spent developing this book, the idea of following the money has deflated significantly. There have, of course, been efforts in the past to delve into the financial mechanisms of certain sections of the CIA, for example, as those sections pertained or could have pertained to the assassination. Jim Garrison's unsuccessful prosecution of Clay Shaw revealed one such piece of the puzzle, albeit many years after the defendant's acquittal. Additionally, in James W. Douglass' book, *JFK and the Unspeakable: Why He Died and Why It Matters*, Douglass writes about a CIA finance officer named Jim Wilcott who had alleged a serious link between Oswald and the CIA in his HSCA testimony.[lxix]

In his testimony, Jim Wilcott, who had "worked in the finance branch of the Tokyo CIA station from 1960 to 1964," had spoken with an individual who "revealed the Oswald connection." This individual was a case officer who supervised agents. Wilcott testified that the case officer said that "Wilcott himself had issued an advance on funds for the CIA's Oswald project." Thoroughly and intelligently probed by Douglass, this plausible connection and its source – Wilcott – were deemed "not worthy of belief" by the HSCA.[lxx]

In pondering the possible, tangible, financial links within the context of the assassination, whether connected to CIA-related operations or, as some researchers have posited, to foreign assassins hired either by someone in the U.S. or internationally, at the end of the day, the entire point becomes moot for one simple reason: there are most certainly no receipts left to follow. Researcher and author J. Gary Shaw agrees. For those hoping to find any concrete signs that could help identify the possible deals made between the planners of the assassination and those who carried it out, it is abundantly clear now that those tracks have been covered up or entirely eradicated. If anything, Shaw notes, contracts and deals like these were likely made in the form of "suitcases full of money," under the table and out of sight.

How would one "follow the money," if there had been any to follow, in any case? Government agencies must maintain a level of transparency, but only to the extent required by law. Who is to say that the documents and records that can be made publicly available have not been doctored or edited in some way? It is an appealing idea, partly for its tangible aspects (checks, receipts, bills), and partly for how simple and easy it would seem. But this author must agree with Shaw; the financial trails leading away from the assassination have long since dried up.

A Parting Thought

"Anyone with a few minutes of spare time can prove that Lee Harvey Oswald was not the lone assassin."

– L. Fletcher Prouty, *JFK: The CIA, Vietnam, and the Plot to Assassinate John F. Kennedy*.

Vietnam

This is, of course, a complicated matter, and one that delves into many topics – from foreign policy and America's political structures to its complicated history and culture. A big question for many researchers has been, would President Kennedy have escalated the fighting in Vietnam had he lived? More talented and knowledgeable people have spent entire careers trying to pin this down. In some ways, it is now relatively useless to try to decipher what President Kennedy *would* have done. That knowledge is hopelessly elusive. But what is not in doubt is that the President's life had ended; the gears of governance continued to turn; the transition of power occurred; and Lyndon Johnson had become President of the United States. The Johnson administration supported several excellent initiatives, including the Civil Rights Act of 1964 and the Voting Rights Act of 1965, both of which were signed into law by President Johnson. But in the days following John Kennedy's death, the "conflict" in Vietnam had become a war.

It is important, as this author has learned, not to conflate Kennedy the man with Kennedy the legend—that iconic ideal of a forward-thinking, modern President. Yet there is plenty of overlap, and that overlap must be considered and evaluated. Kennedy was not perfect, nor was he always a role model, but all of this has been explored as well – by those who knew him, loved him, worked with or under him, and those who fought with him, both politically and ideologically. There are important moments in time when the human being and the legend intersect, such as when, as reflected in various speeches, particularly his commencement address at American University in Washington, D.C., on June 10, 1963, he declared that the people of America, and those of its enemy, the Soviet Union, "all inhabit this small planet."

The President stated: "We all breathe the same air. We all cherish our children's future. And we are all mortal ... Let us reexamine our attitude toward the cold war, remembering that we are not engaged in a debate, seeking to pile up debating points. We are not here distributing blame or pointing the finger of judgment. We must deal with the world as it is, and not as it might have been had the history of the last 18 years been different. We must, therefore, persevere in the search for peace in the hope that constructive changes within the Communist bloc might bring within reach solutions which now seem beyond us. We must conduct our affairs in such a way that it becomes in the Communists' interest to agree on a genuine peace. Above all, while defending our own vital interests, nuclear powers must avert those confrontations which bring an adversary to a choice of either a humiliating retreat or a nuclear war. To adopt that kind of course in the nuclear age would be evidence only of the bankruptcy of our policy — or of a collective death-wish for the world."

President Kennedy's legacy of decisions in the geopolitical arena is, at best, complex. It is a mixture of groundbreaking, nuanced, and peace-forward practices, as well as some stubborn, antiquated, and dangerous decisions. In many ways, President Kennedy really *was* the embodiment of that "New Frontier." However, he was also a product of his time. Richard J. Walton, in his grounded, unbiased examination of President Kennedy's foreign policy, *Cold War and Counter-Revolution: The Foreign Policy of John F. Kennedy*, writes that "After the Moscow Treaty,[*] in the final months of Kennedy's life, even while things were getting worse in Vietnam, they were getting better with the Soviet Union. During the summer the 'hot line,' an emergency communications link, was installed, connecting the White House and the Kremlin ... And at the United Nations on

---

[*] Ratified on October 7, 1963, it prohibited nuclear weapons testing in the atmosphere, underwater, or in outer space.

September 20 he declared, 'If this pause in the Cold War merely leads to its renewal and not its end—then the indictment of posterity will rightly point its finger at us all'"[lxxi]

Among President Kennedy's various supporters and detractors, Walton's voice comes off as one of the most objective and lucid, balancing out the late President's public words, decisions, and policies to reveal a contradictory figure. While it is not a subject of this book, understanding President Kennedy's actions while in office can help researchers, investigators, and the casually curious to gain a deeper understanding of the assassination and the time period in which it happened. As Walton writes, "it is true that five months before his death he publicly recognized, in the American University speech [part of which has been quoted above], that nuclear diplomacy was unacceptably dangerous, but only after he had taken the world to the brink of nuclear war.[*] It is to his lasting credit that he urged the American people to re-examine its attitudes toward the Cold War, but he himself did not understand it and confused the entirely normal competition between the United States and the Soviet Union with the inevitable revolutionary struggle in Asia and Latin America."[lxxii]

---

[*] Walton argues in his book that some of President Kennedy's actions before and during the Cuban Missile Crisis exacerbated tensions among the U.S., the Soviet Union, and Cuba. He lays out several examples, tying them into a large, global perspective while also reexamining the President's stated points of view on various matters and issues.

A combination of the old and the new, John Kennedy was, undeniably, a wholly American individual. Even though his presidency lasted just over 1,000 days, he nevertheless left behind a complicated legacy. Part of his undying popularity —and some of the reasons behind his legacy—lies in what he chose to represent, rather than in what he had accomplished. (For example, while he is often remembered as a staunch proponent of African American Civil Rights, which he was, his successor was the one to sign into law both the Civil Rights Act and the Voting Rights Act.) Near the beginning of his book, Walton muses that "while it is true, and good, that Kennedy learned from the missile crisis, he had more to learn."[lxxiii] His leadership and example were tragically cut short; it is also tragic, for all Americans, that Kennedy's presidency was replaced not through the democratic process but through rifle fire. Many people, even now, cannot help but wonder what could have been had President Kennedy lived long enough to complete his first term – or even to ascend to a second.

Cold Case

As is apparent from the content and sources in this book, the author did not work off a "bombshell" new piece of evidence, a long-lost clue, or something else as salacious, exciting, and, perhaps in some cases, misleading. Everything here is "old news," particularly for those familiar with the assassination and those who have done deep dives into the smaller, more self-contained aspects of the narrative. Some might, in all fairness, call this effort a pointless retread. That is a familiar stance to this author. But, in the end, the research was done, and the book was finished anyway.

Never promising or hinting at any definitive answers, the object of this book is to approach the assassination from a sociological perspective, examining how the mainstream news media and journalism have shaped our understanding and perception of what is surely one of the most important events in America's history. As a powerful tool for information and interpretation, the fourth estate was chosen as a worthy starting point for a new exploration of a topic that has been looked at from many other vantage points.

William Walter's story has persistently intrigued, puzzled, and aggravated this author. If only a copy of the teletype had been made—by anyone. Walter repeatedly stated that his intention was to write down the message, not to keep a copy of a government document. Is there, perhaps, a hidden copy of the teletype made by another employee of the New Orleans office, undisclosed all this time? Since Jim Garrison's appearance on *The Tonight Show*, it really *has* become a "phantom" teletype, as the FBI derisively called it. Like many aspects of the larger story, Walter's account is full of unanswered questions, however small they may be in comparison to the bigger ones.

As must be clear by this point, this author does not subscribe to the Oswald-did-it theory. It is resoundingly redundant and has been more than adequately disproved. The fatal shot that struck President Kennedy in the head had come from in front of the motorcade. There was more than one shooter involved. Individuals in the federal government, to varying degrees, participated in the cover-up (or even multiple cover-ups) following the assassination. None of this is new. Ultimately, it does not matter what this author thinks about the culprits, the possible motives, or who fired the kill shot. The result is always the same: a President of the United States was gunned down in the street, in broad daylight, in full view of spectators and passersby, in cold blood. Where can one go from here? Where does America go? Where *did* it go after November 22, 1963? These are all enormous questions, far outside the scope of this little book – but they are yours, now, to ponder.

This is far from an "active investigation." In a sense, this book, and the research community at large, constitute a "picking up of the pieces," setting some aspects of the story straight while highlighting, to a greater degree than before, others. This may sound like a pessimistic appraisal, and perhaps it is, but it is by no means a call to surrender, to wind down, or to give in. This has always been, and will continue to be, an effort for truth – the total, complete truth. While there may not be one final capital "T" truth in the end – one that finally makes sense of all the disparate pieces – the smaller truths are still worth it, all the same.

History Repeats

"What if hundreds of millions of people believe in 'a reality' that is actually a lie? What if that false reality was intentionally created as part of a political agenda that resulted in seizing state power and changed the course of history? And if the unseen forces behind all this could change the past and get away with it, if they could convince all of America to believe in a false history that concealed acts of treason and enormous political crimes, didn't that mean they could shape the future?"

That quote is from Craig Unger's brilliant book, *Den of Spies: Reagan, Carter, and the Secret History of the Treason That Stole the White House*. Likely not the kind of book to be referenced in this context. Although those words deal with an entirely different event in our history – the "October Surprise," a covert plot involving hostages, illicit weapons sales, and a cover-up that ensured Ronald Reagan's presidential victory over Jimmy Carter in 1981 – Unger's remarks echo the core issue at the heart of President Kennedy's assassination. With that assessment, published just recently in 2024, comes the terrible, sinking feeling that history is repeating itself. There also comes the terrible feeling of a near-total lack of control. This author believes in the efficacy of voting in our democracy, but certain events, however old or shadowy, often put one's trust in our representative democracy in serious doubt.

It is then both a tiring reality and an invitation to participate more actively in our own lives that human history is not automatically defined or characterized by facts or the truth. As this book demonstrates, the news media, as an industry and as a cultural establishment, remain a key component of the process through which history forms. The fourth estate functions in a capacity that is both unique and double-edged: it can support and defend people's liberties within a democracy, and it can also construct dishonest and poisonous narratives that negatively affect both history and democracy. It is, however, an "estate" that responds to the people, that can be made to work better, and with greater honesty and independence from fear or favor.

The news media do not exist in isolation from any other aspect of society, removed from the world and the people in it. Just as voting in local, state, and national elections plays a crucial role in the American experiment – a system that works better the more people participate – a more involved and attentive audience empowers a kind of journalism that is more responsive to the needs of the people. This involvement can ultimately develop into a thriving, more responsible news media – one that better serves democracy and its people. Changes like this, whether in the fabric of journalism or in the inner workings of government, do not happen constructively and peacefully overnight. As discussed earlier, on a more personal level, consumers can learn to better engage with the news, thereby not only avoiding the effects of bias – intended or otherwise – but also getting more out of the news they read, watch, or listen to. In a broader sense, it must be remembered that the news media, like any business, eventually answer to consumer demands.

In recent years, traditional news media, now often referred to as "legacy media," have faced criticism from smaller, independent programs and publications, with various commentators and broadcasters pointing out the stagnation readily apparent in much of their output. This stagnation is a major reason many turn to social media, YouTube, and podcasts for their news and current events. This is also why many corporations in the traditional media sphere, spanning the political and social divides, have been forced to spend much of their energy and time becoming more marketable and accessible – often at the cost of effective, unbiased, and responsible journalism.

Just as the fourth estate remains inextricably linked to many other functions and aspects of daily life, so too does the assassination of President Kennedy continue to permeate American culture, history, and society. His murder was not approached or reported on in an isolated manner; looking at the way in which the news agencies of the time characterized President Kennedy's death, as well as the subsequent murder of Lee Harvey Oswald and the different investigations that followed, has revealed a dangerous and almost self-perpetuating bias. This bias, especially towards Oswald's *alleged* guilt, has sadly and unjustly stood the test of time, revealing the frail and precarious viability of responsible journalism in this country. This author has sought to showcase this in a simple, accessible manner, tying together and analyzing those things which had already been linked for a long, long time: the assassination of John F. Kennedy and the American news media.

"The people are the only censors of their governors: and even their errors will tend to keep these to the true principles of their institution. To punish these errors too severely would be to suppress the only safeguard of the public liberty. The way to prevent these irregular interpositions of the people is to give them full information of their affairs thro' the channel of the public papers, and to contrive that those papers should penetrate the whole mass of the people. The basis of our governments being the opinion of the people, the very first object should be to keep that right; and were it left to me to decide whether we should have a government without newspapers, or newspapers without a government, I should not hesitate a moment to prefer the latter."

– Thomas Jefferson, from a letter to Edward Carrington, January 16, 1787.

AN AUTHOR'S JOURNEY

This final section is purely subjective. It is a brief reflection on why and how this project came to be. I owe a great deal to what I consider to be an American epic: Oliver Stone's *JFK*. Among the films that ignited my interest in American history, the extended director's cut stands shoulder to shoulder with *All the President's Men*, *Mississippi Burning*, and *Judgment at Nuremberg*. In my mind, these are historical films that go beyond history; stories that attempt to achieve an honest impression of a particular moment in time.

JFK was my introduction to the assassination, a topic that I would soon learn constitutes its own vast universe. It would be many years after watching and rewatching the film before I would take a serious interest in the subject. The book that first pushed me into the deep end of this pool was Dr. Charles Crenshaw's *JFK: Conspiracy of Silence*. Finding a paperback copy for about a dollar at a used bookstore – written by a doctor who was *there*, who had seen both the President and Lee Harvey Oswald mortally wounded, dying – I bought it, read it in a few days, and the rest, as they say, was history. After Dr. Crenshaw's book, I quickly followed up with Henry Hurt's authoritative *Reasonable Doubt*, then Jim Marrs' exhaustive *Crossfire*, and many, many others since. (*Crossfire* was one of the two books that made up the historical basis for Stone's *JFK*; the other was Jim Garrison's *On the Trail of the Assassins*, a book I read fervently.)

I never had plans to write a book, do any serious digging, or reach out to assassination researchers and talk to them one-on-one. Sometimes, life makes its own plans. Having finished *Reasonable Doubt*, I decided, what the heck, let me see if I could find Henry on Facebook. After striking up a conversation with him online, I would end up visiting him several times to talk about many things: the assassination itself, of course, as well as the resulting cover-up; the enigma that was Oswald; my nascent (at the time) book; the 2025 declassified documents; and much more.

Through Henry, I got in touch with J. Gary Shaw, an assassination researcher who has been tracking the case for decades (and, as it happens, was a co-author of *JFK: Conspiracy of Silence*). My first talk with Gary was short but rewarding. He noted, and I agreed, that a "Big Truth" about the President's death will likely never be discovered. Nevertheless, Gary stressed the importance of continuing the search and sharing what one learns with other researchers. Gary's initial words of encouragement are a big part of why this book was made. My visits with Henry and my phone calls with Gary have meant a lot to me. It has been nothing short of a privilege to talk with them, learn from them, and share intermittent progress updates throughout the development of this book. On that note, I would be horribly remiss not to include a note of thanks to my publisher, Dr. Michael Marcades. He guided me through a completely new process. I would email him with questions, and he willingly answered them with support and good humor. His invaluable assistance made this, my first book, a reality.

While it has been several years since I worked full-time as a journalist, I have continued to write freelance for different publications. In fact, becoming a journalist had been a dream of mine since a young age, the blame for which must be placed entirely on my dad. At what must have been a fairly impressionable age, he introduced me to *Kolchak: The Night Stalker*, a mid-70s TV show focusing on a frazzled but determined Chicago reporter named Carl Kolchak who, invariably, would face off with a different monster or supernatural creature every week. To this day, I still love the show and revisit it on occasion. Kolchak, brought to life by veteran actor Darren McGavin (the dad from *A Christmas Story*), brought an underdog's passion and gumption to the series, even when some episodes were, however, goofy. If *All the President's Men* was a kind of chilling wake-up call, *Kolchak: The Night Stalker* gave me the reporter's bug. In addition to the ink and newsprint, journalism was a constant fight for truth (with or without the werewolves, zombies, and vampires).

During my time as a reporter, I covered everything from local politics and music festivals to the daily trials and tribulations of small business owners. This left a massive impression on me; the printed word *can* make a difference, however small. I can attest to this firsthand. The story I am most proud of to this day: a spotlight on a small restaurant – that had once been a food truck – and was, at the time, at risk of losing its certificate of occupancy, something it needed to maintain its "brick and mortar" location. While I am sure that my story did not singlehandedly keep the restaurant from closing its door, it was a rewarding experience, anyway – to interview the owners, get their side of the story (the municipal owners of the property had not been communicating clearly with the restaurant's proprietors), and highlight how difficult and even precarious it can be to operate a small business. (To this day, the restaurant is still open.)

Deciding to reexamine the assassination through a reporter's lens, the subsequent months of writing, editing, and rewriting have been a journey – both figuratively and literally. My visits to Henry took up several hours each way, and at one point, I felt compelled to venture out to the National Archives at College Park, Maryland, to supplement my online research.

In what almost feels like a past life, I used to spend a good deal of time writing poetry. (I have had an odd poem published here and there, which has always felt nice.) Coming from more of an artistic background, I never expected to write a book like this – much less a book that focused on a subject as involved and, at times, controversial as President Kennedy's assassination. I could, of course, blame Oliver Stone for getting me into this – but I will not do that. Instead, I will close this final, rambling chapter with a sincere and massive "Thank you" to everyone who helped me in ways large and small – from pointing me in the right direction to taking the time to speak with me and help me understand aspects of the assassination that I had not previously considered.

Lastly, I want to thank anyone who has ever dared to probe for the truth; to understand Lee Harvey Oswald's tragic place in this story; and to help America at large acknowledge that

President Kennedy's assassination, more than six decades after the fact, continues to be as misinterpreted, mischaracterized, and as culturally and historically significant as it was on November 22, 1963.

The old adage is true: the more things change, the more they stay the same.

RESOURCES

Cited Books

In alphabetical order, by title.

Cold War and Counter-Revolution: The Foreign Policy of John F. Kennedy, Richard J. Walton. The Viking Press, Inc., 1972 hardcover edition.

Crossfire: The Plot That Killed Kennedy by Jim Marrs. Carroll & Graf Publishers, Inc., 1990 paperback edition.

A Farewell to Justice: Jim Garrison, JFK's Assassination, and the Case That Should Have Changed History by Joan Mellen. Potomac Books, Inc. 2007 paperback ed.

A Heritage of Stone by Jim Garrison. G.P. Putnam's Sons. 1970 hardcover ed.

JFK: The CIA, Vietnam, and the Plot to Assassinate John F. Kennedy by L. Fletcher Prouty. Skyhorse Publishing. 2011 paperback ed.

JFK: Conspiracy of Silence by Charles A. Crenshaw, MD, with Jens Hansen and J. Gary Shaw. Signet, Published by the Penguin Group. 1992 paperback ed.

JFK and the Unspeakable: Why He Died and Why It Matters by James W. Douglass. Touchstone, A Division of Simon & Schuster, Inc. 2008 paperback ed.

The Last Investigation by Gaeton Fonzi. Mary Ferrell Foundation Press. 2008 paperback ed.

On the Trail of the Assassins: One Man's Quest to Solve the Murder of President Kennedy by Jim Garrison. Skyhorse Publishing. 2012 ed.

Oswald Talked: The New Evidence in the JFK Assassination by Ray and Mary LaFontaine. Pelican Publishing Company. 1996 hardcover ed.

Reasonable Doubt: An Investigation into the Assassination of John F. Kennedy by Henry Hurt. Holt, Rinehart and Winston. 1986 hardcover ed.

Rush To Judgment: A Critique of the Warren Commission's Inquiry into the Murders of President John F. Kennedy, Officer J.D. Tippit and Lee Harvey Oswald by Mark Lane. Holt, Rinehart & Winston. 1966 hardcover ed.

The Texas Connection by Craig I. Zirbel. Warner Books, Inc. 1992 paperback ed.

Trauma Room One: The JFK Medical Coverup Exposed by Charles A. Crenshaw, MD, with J. Gary Shaw, D. Bradley Kizzia, JD, Gary Aguilar, MD, and Cyril Wecht, MD, JD. Paraview Press, 2001 paperback ed.

Cited Articles
In chronological order of publication.

New York *Herald Tribune* – Sunday, November 23, 1963. (Vol. CXXII, I No. 42,611.)

The *Danville Register* – Saturday, November 23, 1963. (No. 26, 252.)

New York *Herald Tribune* – Monday, November 25, 1963. (Vol. CXXIII, No. 42,613.)

"Garrison Claims Oswald Tipped FBI." *The Dallas Morning News*. December 27, 1967.

"FBI Chiefs Linked To Oswald File Loss" by Martin Waldron. *The New York Times*. September 17, 1975.

Morgan City Daily Review, "Walter Reveals Prior Warning On Potential JFK Assassination,"
October 1, 1975.

"The Single-Assassin Theory, the Media Establishment and the CIA" by Donald E. Wilkes, Jr. Digital Commons, University of Georgia, School of Law. Originally published in *Flagpole* Magazine. November 23, 2016.

"Did J. Edgar Hoover Kill JFK?" by Donald E. Wilkes, Jr. Digital Commons, University of Georgia, School of Law. Originally published in *Flagpole* Magazine. December 27, 2017.

"The Real Story of the Assassination of Robert F. Kennedy" by Donald E. Wilkes, Jr. *Flagpole* Magazine (www.flagpole.com). June 19, 2019.

Erroneous Articles
In chronological order of publication.

"What We Know and Still Don't Know About JFK's Assassination" by Olivia B. Waxman. November 21, 2023. *Time Magazine.*

"JFK assassination remembered 60 years later by surviving witnesses to history, including AP reporter" by Jamie Stengle. November 22, 2023. AP News.

"John F. Kennedy Assassination Fast Facts," CNN Editorial Research. October 30, 2024. CNN.

"More details about JFK assassination keep emerging, even 61 years later" by Elizabeth Weise. November 22, 2024. USA Today.

Online Resources

A note of gratitude to the Mary Ferrell Foundation, Inc. (www.maryferrell.org), which remains the premier, most accessible, and free online resource for assassination researchers at all levels, from those just starting out to those who have dedicated their lives to the task. Rex Bradford, of the Mary Ferrell Foundation, deserves a special note of thanks, as he kindly answered this author's questions

174

throughout the creation of this book. Many of the photographs and document scans used in these pages were obtained courtesy of the Foundation.

Articles/Pages
In order of usage in the text.

Mary Ferrell Foundation (www.maryferrell.org). Online article, "Witnesses."

Britannica (www.britannica.com). Online article, "Assassination of John F. Kennedy."

Vanderbilt News Archive (www.tvnews.vanderbilt.edu). Online page, "John F. Kennedy Assassination/Warren Commission/Walter/FBI – #242197."

History, Art & Archives – United States House of Representatives (www.history.house.gov). Online article, "The Disappearance of Majority Leader Hale Boggs of Louisiana and Representative Nicholas Begich of Alaska."

A Note on Government Records and Sources

Of all the various government records and memoranda that I researched and explored online, primarily through the Mary Ferrell Foundation, as well as other public online sources, and in-person at the National Archives in College Park, Maryland, the following were the most pertinent and elemental in terms of piecing together a cohesive chronology for Walter's story. These documents, as well as Walter's

HSCA deposition, helped reconstruct the basic order of events, the core of his allegation regarding the teletype, and represented a consistent (and negative) response on the part of the FBI and Department of Justice regarding Walter.

Memoranda

Memorandum, U.S. Secret Service, Protective Research Section, San Antonio Office, Texas. Date of origin: November 15, 1963.

Memo, Federal Bureau of Investigation (FBI), Jacksonville Office, Florida. Re: Assassination of President John Fitzgerald Kennedy. February 2, 1968.

Informative Note, Domestic Intelligence Division, FBI. March 22, 1968. Accessed at the National Archives in College Park, Maryland.

Memo, FBI, New Orleans Office, Louisiana. Re: Assassination of President John Fitzgerald Kennedy. April 1, 1968.

Memo to W.C. Sullivan, from W.A. Branigan. Re: Assassination of President John Fitzgerald Kennedy. May 3, 1968.

Memo to Fred M. Vinson, Jr., Assistant Attorney General, from Director, FBI. Re: Assassination of President John Fitzgerald Kennedy. May 3, 1968.

Memo to Fred M. Vinson, Jr., Assistant Attorney General, from Director, FBI. Re: Assassination of President John Fitzgerald Kennedy. December 23, 1968.

Memo to Mr. Gallagher, from B. H. Cooke, FBI. September 11, 1975. Accessed at the National Archives in College Park, Maryland.

Memo to Mr. Gallagher, from B. H. Cooke, FBI. September 30, 1975. Accessed at the National Archives in College Park, Maryland.

Memo to Mr. Gallagher, from B. H. Cooke, FBI. October 1, 1975. Accessed at the National Archives in College Park, Maryland.

Government Testimonies and Reports

Report of the President's Commission on the Assassination of President John F. Kennedy (the "Warren Report"). September 27, 1964.

Hearings Before the President's Commission on the Assassination of President Kennedy. November 23, 1964.

Subcommittee on Civil and Constitutional Rights, Committee on the Judiciary, House of Representatives. "Circumstances Surrounding Destruction of the Lee Harvey Oswald Note." December 12, 1975.

House Select Committee on Assassinations, Final Report, Part I: Findings of the Select Committee on Assassination in the Assassination of President John F. Kennedy. December 30, 1978.

House Select Committee on Assassinations, Subcommittee on the Assassination of John F. Kennedy. Deposition of William S. Walter. March 23, 1978.

Photographs and Visual Examples

Unless otherwise noted, all the photographs and scanned documents included in this book are in the public domain, obtained courtesy of the Mary Ferrell Foundation, Inc.

Aerial View of Dealey Plaza. Warren Commission Report, Public Domain. Obtained via Wikimedia Commons (www.commons.wikimedia.org).

Polaroid photograph taken just after the fatal headshot struck President John F. Kennedy, November 22, 1963. Mary Ann Moorman, Public Domain. Obtained via Wikimedia Commons (www.commons.wikimedia.org).

Warren Commission Exhibit 762. Warren Commission Report, Public Domain. Obtained via GovInfo (www.govinfo.gov).

ENDNOTES

PART ONE: THE ASSASSINATION AND THE MEDIA ESTABLISHMENT

[i] *Crossfire: The Plot That Killed Kennedy*, Jim Marrs, p. 69.

[ii] *Reasonable Doubt: An Investigation into the Assassination of John F. Kennedy*, Henry Hurt, p. 129.
[iii] *The Texas Connection,* Craig I. Zirbel, p. 33.

[iv] Ibid., pp. 48, 54.

[v] *Rush To Judgment: A Critique of the Warren Commission's Inquiry into the Murders of President John F. Kennedy, Officer J.D. Tippit and Lee Harvey Oswald* by Mark Lane, p. 38.

[vi] Ibid., p. 41.

[vii] AP News, Jamie Stengle.

[viii] *JFK: Conspiracy of Silence*, Charles Crenshaw, MD, with Jens Hansen and J. Gary Shaw. p. 112.

[ix] Ibid.

[x] Ibid.

[xi] *Rush To Judgment: A Critique of the Warren Commission's Inquiry into the Murders of President John F. Kennedy,*

Officer J.D. Tippit and Lee Harvey Oswald by Mark Lane, p. 46.

[xii] Ibid., pp. 46 - 47.

[xiii] Ibid., p. 51.

[xiv] *Trama Room One: The JFK Medical Coverup Exposed*, Charles A. Crenshaw, MD, with J. Gary Shaw, D. Bradley Kizzia, JD, Gary Aguilar, MD, and Cyril Wecht, MD, JD, p. 185.

[xv] Ibid.

[xvi] Ibid., p. 194.

[xvii] Ibid., pp. 200 - 202.

[xviii] Ibid., p. 237.

[xix] *Rush To Judgment: A Critique of the Warren Commission's Inquiry into the Murders of President John F. Kennedy, Officer J.D. Tippit and Lee Harvey Oswald* by Mark Lane, p. 47.

[xx] Ibid., p. 52.

[xxi] *JFK: Conspiracy of Silence*, Charles Crenshaw, MD, with Jens Hansen and J. Gary Shaw, p. 132.

xxii Ibid., p. 137.

PART TWO: WILLIAM S. WALTER AND THE PHANTOM TELETYPE

xxiii William S. Walter, Deposition, Select Committee on Assassinations, March 23, 1978, and Memo to Fred Vinson, Jr., FBI, 5/3/1968.

xxiv *Oswald Talked: The New Evidence in the JFK Assassination* by Ray and Mary LaFontaine. Pelican Publishing Company. 1996 hardcover ed.

xxv Memo to Fred M. Vinson, Jr., Assistant Attorney General, from Director, FBI. FBI, Re: Assassination of President John Fitzgerald Kennedy, November 22, 1963, Dallas, Texas. December 23, 1968.

xxvi Memo to Mr. Gallagher, from B. H. Cooke, FBI. October 1, 1975, and *On the Trail of the Assassins*, Jim Garrison, p. 221.

xxvii "Walter Reveals Prior Warning On Potential JFK Assassination," Morgan City *Daily Review*, 10/1/75.

xxviii Memo, Federal Bureau of Investigation (FBI), Jacksonville Office, Florida. Re: Assassination of President John Fitzgerald Kennedy. February 2, 1968.

xxix Ibid.

xxx Ibid.

xxxi Memo to W.C. Sullivan, from W.A. Branigan. Re: Assassination of President John Fitzgerald Kennedy. May 3, 1968.

xxxii William S. Walter, Deposition, (HSCA), March 23, 1978, and Memo to Fred Vinson, Jr., FBI, 5/3/1968.

xxxiii Memo to Mr. Gallagher, from B. H. Cooke, FBI. September 11, 1975.

xxxiv Memo to Fred M. Vinson, Jr., Assistant Attorney General, from Director, FBI. Re: Assassination of President John Fitzgerald Kennedy. May 3, 1968.
xxxv William S. Walter, Deposition, HSCA, p 34.

xxxvi *Conspiracy*, Anthony Summers, 1980 edition, pp. 301 - 311.

xxxvii Memo to Fred M. Vinson, Jr., Assistant Attorney General, from Director, FBI. FBI, Re: Assassination of President John Fitzgerald Kennedy. December 23, 1968.

xxxviii Memo, FBI, New Orleans Office, Louisiana. Re: Assassination of President John Fitzgerald Kennedy. April 1, 1968.

xxxix Memo to the Attorney General from Director, FBI. Re: Assassination of President John Fitzgerald Kennedy, November 22, 1963, Dallas, Texas. April 4, 1968.

xl William S. Walter, Deposition, HSCA, p. 40.
xli *Crossfire*, Marrs, p. 228.

xlii House Select Committee on Assassinations, Final Report, Part I, Findings, C, p. 192.

xliii Subcommittee on Civil and Constitutional Rights, Committee on the Judiciary, House of Representatives. "Circumstances Surrounding Destruction of the Lee Harvey Oswald Note," pp. 167 - 168.

xliv Ibid.

xlv William S. Walter, Deposition, (HSCA), March 23, 1978, p. 12.
xlvi Ibid., pp. 12 - 13.

xlvii *On the Trail of the Assassins*, Garrison, p. 221.

xlviii Deposition, HSCA, p. 31.

xlix Ibid.

l Ibid., pp. 32 - 33.

li Ibid., p. 39.

[lii] Ibid., p. 40.

[liii] Ibid., p. 38.

[liv] Ibid., pp. 49 - 50.
[lv] Ibid., p. 50.

[lvi] Ibid., p. 68.

[lvii] Informative Note, Domestic Intelligence Division, FBI. 3/22/68.

[lviii] Memo to Mr. Gallagher, from B. H. Cooke, 9/30/75.

[lix] Vanderbilt News Archive (www.tvnews.vanderbilt.edu). "John F. Kennedy Assassination / Warren Commission / Walter / FBI – #242197."

[lx] Ibid.

[lxi] Transcript of Taped Interview of William S. Walter, 10/1/75, on WGSO Radio, New Orleans, LA. Mary Ferrell Foundation.

[lxii] History, Art & Archives – United States House of Representatives (www.history.house.gov). Online article, "The Disappearance of Majority Leader Hale Boggs of Louisiana and Representative Nicholas Begich of Alaska."

[lxiii] Ibid.

[lxiv] *Reasonable Doubt: An Investigation into the Assassination of John F. Kennedy*, Henry Hurt, pp. 193 - 194.

PART THREE: A PLACE IN HISTORY

[lxv] *The Last Investigation*, Gaeton Fonzi, p. 29.

[lxvi] *A Heritage of Stone*, Jim Garrison, p. 210.

[lxvii] Ibid., p. 211.

[lxviii] Ibid., p. 215.

[lxix] *JFK and the Unspeakable: Why He Died and Why It Matters*, James W. Douglass, p. 146.

[lxx] Ibid., p. 421.

[lxxi] *Cold War and Counter-Revolution: The Foreign Policy of John F. Kennedy*, Richard J. Walton, p. 159.

[lxxii] Ibid., 233.

[lxxiii] Ibid., pp. 144 - 145.

www.ingramcontent.com/pod-product-compliance
Lightning Source LLC
Chambersburg PA
CBHW060517130626

46553CB00002B/536